OVERTUI

MW00653119

in association with

We are delighted to have the opportunity to work with Overture Publishing on this series of opera guides and to build on the work English National Opera did over twenty years ago on the Calder Opera Guide Series. As well as reworking and updating existing titles, Overture and ENO have commissioned new titles for the series and all of the guides will be published to coincide with repertoire being staged by the company at the London Coliseum.

This volume is published to mark a major new production at ENO of *The Flying Dutchman*, directed by Jonathan Kent and conducted by ENO Music Director Edward Gardner. The cast is led by James Creswell in the title role, with Orla Boylan as Senta, Stuart Skelton as Erik and Clive Bayley as Daland.

We hope that these guides will prove an invaluable resource now and for years to come, and that by delving deeper into the history of an opera, the poetry of the libretto and the nuances of the score, readers' understanding and appreciation of the opera and the art form in general will be enhanced.

John Berry
Artistic Director, ENO
April 2012

The publisher John Calder began the Opera Guides series under the editorship of the late Nicholas John in association with English National Opera in 1980. It ran until 1994 and eventually included forty-eight titles, covering fifty-eight operas. The books in the series were intended to be companions to the works that make up the core of the operatic repertory. They contained articles, illustrations, musical examples and a complete libretto and singing translation of each opera in the series, as well as bibliographies and discographies.

The aim of the present relaunched series is to make available again the guides already published in a redesigned format with new illustrations, some newly commissioned articles, updated reference sections and a literal translation of the libretto that will enable the reader to get closer to the intentions and meaning of the original. New guides of operas not already covered will be published alongside the redesigned ones from the old series.

Gary Kahn
Series Editor

Der fliegende Holländer

Richard Wagner

Overture Opera Guides
Series Editor
Gary Kahn

Editorial Consultant
Philip Reed
Head of Publications, ENO

OVERTURE

OVERTURE OPERA GUIDES
in association with

Overture Publishing
an imprint of

ALMA CLASSICS LTD
London House
243–253 Lower Mortlake Road
Richmond
Surrey TW9 2LL
United Kingdom

Articles by John Warrack, John Deathridge and William Vaughan first published
by John Calder (Publishers) Ltd
© the authors, 1982

Articles by Mike Ashman and Katherine Syer first published in this volume
© the authors, 2012

Translations from Wagner's prose writings by Melanie Karpinski
© the author, 1982

This *Der fliegende Holländer* Opera Guide first published by Overture Publishing,
an imprint of Alma Classics Ltd, 2012

© Alma Classics Ltd, 2012
All rights reserved

Translation of libretto © Lionel Salter Library, www.lionelsalter.co.uk
Reprinted by kind permission of Graham Salter

Cover image: Peter West/Donnington Arts

Printed in Great Britain by TJ International, Padstow, Cornwall
Typeset by Tetragon

ISBN: 978-1-84749-549-5

Contents

List of Illustrations

1. Richard Wagner, drawing begun in 1840 by Ernst Kietz and finished by him in 1842, the year before the premiere of *Der fliegende Holländer*.

2. The poet Heinrich Heine in 1842, drawing by Samuel Friedrich Diez (above).
3. The Royal Saxon Court Theatre, Dresden, where *Der fliegende Holländer*
was first performed, lithograph, *c*.1840 (below).

Engravings from the Leipzig *Illustrirte Zeitung*, 7th October 1843, of the first performances in Dresden: 4. The Dutchman (top left); 5. Senta (top right); 6. The final scene of Act Three (below).

7. Set design for Act Two of the first Bayreuth Festival production in 1901, directed by Cosima Wagner and designed by Max Brückner. An insistence on Scandinavian naturalism (above). 8. The Royal Opera House, Berlin production in 1909. Anton van Rooy (right) as the Dutchman at the end of Act Three. The cast in authentically Nordic costumes (below).

9. Set design by Anton Briosci based on ones by Alfred Roller for the Court Opera, Vienna production in 1913. A move away from strict naturalism (above).
10. Moje Forbach as Senta, Martin Abendroth as Daland and Fritz Krenn as the Dutchman in the Krolloper production that Otto Klemperer conducted in 1929, directed by Jürgen Fehling and designed by Ewald Dülberg. The expressionist break with the past that led to the Nazis closing the opera house (below).

The Dutchman and Senta in the twentieth century:
11. Leonie Rysanek and George London (top left); 12. Gré Brouwenstijn and Leonard Wolovsky (top right); 13. David Ward and Gwyneth Jones (bottom left); 14. José van Dam and Hildegard Behrens (bottom right).

15. Astrid Varnay as Senta in the production directed and designed by Wolfgang Wagner at the Bayreuth Festival in 1955 (above). 16. Anja Silja as Senta and Thomas Stewart as the Dutchman in the production directed and designed by Wieland Wagner at the Bayreuth Festival, first seen in 1959, here in 1965 (below).

17. Joachim Herz's production, designed by Rudolf Heinrich, at the Komische Oper in 1962. Christa-Maria Ziese as Senta (above). 18. Clifford Williams's production, with the rotating hydraulic set designed by Sean Kenny, at the Royal Opera House, first seen in 1966, here in 1972 (below).

19. The production directed and designed by Jean-Pierre Ponnelle
at San Francisco Opera in 1975 (above). 20. Ulrich Melchinger's production,
designed by Thomas Richter-Forgách, at the Staatstheater Kassel in 1976.
Edgar Keenon, centre, as the Dutchman (below).

21. Harry Kupfer's production, designed by Peter Sykora, at the Bayreuth
Festival in 1978. Lisbeth Balslev as Senta and Anny Schlemm as Mary.

22. The production directed and designed by Herbert Wernicke at the Bayerische Staatsoper in 1981. Franz Ferdinand Nentwig as the Dutchman (above).

23. David Pountney's production, designed by Stefanos Lazaridis at ENO in 1982. Josephine Barstow as Senta and Norman Bailey as the Dutchman (below).

24. David Pountney's production, designed by Stefanos Lazaridis, on the shores of Lake Constance at the Bregenz Festival in 1989 (above).
25. The production directed and designed by Willy Decker at Oper Köln in 1991. Josef Protschka as Erik and Lisbeth Balslev as Senta (below).

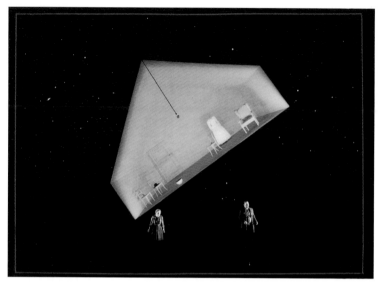

26. Dieter Dorn's production, designed by Jürgen Rose, at the Bayreuth
Festival in 1992. Daland's house making its 360-degree turn in Act Two.
Sabine Hass as Senta and Bernd Weikl as the Dutchman (above).
27. Richard Jones's production, designed by Nigel Lowery, at De Nederlandse
Opera in 1993. Kathryn Harries, in white, as Senta (below).

28. Peter Konwitschny's production, designed by Johannes Leiacker, at the Bayerische Staatsoper in 2006. Anja Kampe as Senta on an exercise bicycle (above). 29. Calixto Beito's production, designed by Susanne Gschwender and Rebecca Ringst, at Oper Stuttgart in 2008. The Act Three choruses (below).

30. Bryn Terfel as the Dutchman in Tim Albery's production, designed by
Michael Levine, at the Royal Opera House in 2009 (above).
31. Martin Kušej's production, designed by Martin Zehetgruber, at
De Nederlandse Opera in 2010. The end of Act Three with Juha Uusitalo as the
Dutchman, now dead, Catherine Naglestad as Senta (below).

Behind *Der fliegende Holländer*

John Warrack

Wagner was fortunate to grow up in Dresden. As a child there, from 1814 to 1828, he overlapped with the period of Carl Maria von Weber's time as Kapellmeister of the Dresden Opera; his stepfather Ludwig Geyer was an actor and *buffo* tenor in the German company, his sisters sang in Weber's *Preciosa* and (later in Leipzig) *Silvana*, and he himself as a child appeared in one of Weber's occasional pieces, dressed up as an angel with wings sewn onto his back. He had already been spellbound by the figure of the frail Weber limping off to rehearsals, associating physical disability and the creative spark in his mind; and he later wrote, 'In particular [*Der*] *Freischütz* [1821], though mainly because of its spooky plot, affected my imagination with characteristic intensity.'[1] Among his earliest influences were two of the strains that later met in *Der fliegende Holländer,* the work that was in 1843 to give German Romantic opera new maturity: a lure towards the supernatural, and a wide knowledge of the operas that, especially in the repertory of Weber's German company in Dresden, were a creative basis for German Romantic opera.

Wagner seems never completely to have lost the enjoyment of the supernatural that was a fashion in his youth. Having absorbed the atmosphere of the novels of the so-called *Schauerromantik*, or 'Horror Romanticism', he wrote as his first creative effort a drama, *Leubald* (1827–28), which he described with ironic amusement in his autobiography as an absurd farrago of Shakespeare and Goethe,

---

1   Richard Wagner, *My Life*, trans. Andrew Gray, ed. Mary Whittall (Cambridge: Cambridge University Press, 1983), p. 13.

thronged with menacing ghosts. 'The spirit world had a very real meaning for me,' he wrote, and this was in connection with a sound that was to haunt him all his life, the fifths on the open strings of an orchestra tuning up. Whatever the reason, it seized his imagination as 'a greeting from the spirit world'; the tremolo fifths opening Beethoven's Ninth Symphony sent shudders down his spine, and he was to reproduce them (he copied the whole score of the Ninth, and made a piano reduction) as the opening of his own youthful C major Symphony. This was hardly more than direct aural stimulus; that Wagner had also absorbed the dramatic import of the sound, as it struck his imagination, is shown at the beginning of the *Der fliegende Holländer* Overture, where the barren fifths, neither major nor minor even in the horn call that storms through them, suggest a realm beyond such human definitions.

Wagner's absorption in the world of the supernatural was to take manifold forms. Like all his generation, he thrilled to the stories of E.T.A. Hoffmann. 'Now came the time when I really lived and breathed in Hoffmann's artistic atmosphere of ghosts and spirits,' he recalled of his childhood years in his autobiography *Mein Leben* (My Life); a tale that particularly impressed him as a boy was Hoffmann's *Der Magnetiseur* (The Mesmerist, 1814). Together with the readings of Shakespeare, Calderón, Goethe and other great masters that occupied the evenings at Wahnfried, Wagner and Cosima's house in Bayreuth, a place was regularly found for ghost stories; and though concerned not to frighten Cosima, he once badly upset her with his vivid reading of the ghost story *Das Majorat* (Primogeniture, 1817). His projected first opera, *Die Hochzeit* (The Wedding, 1832), was sketched under the influence of Hoffmann, as he admitted; and he first came to know the story of the song contest at the Wartburg, part of the *Tannhäuser* plot, from Hoffmann's treatment of it. He was also, as a young man in Vienna, to take delight in the comedies of Ferdinand Raimund, whose inordinately popular pieces dealt often with the humour of transferring a plain Viennese citizen to the world of spirits, usually for the correction of his faults. Wagner praised Raimund's work in an essay, 'Über Schauspieler und Sänger' (On Actors and Singers); and a diary entry by Cosima, following reading of Raimund, gives as the Wahnfried view that within the bounds of the Viennese popular theatre he was 'an incomparable genius'. There is a line to be traced from these amiable plays, tinged with moral content, to the world of Wagner's first completed opera, *Die Feen* (The Fairies, 1833), and even beyond.

However, subtler ideas on the contact of the human and spirit worlds were also at work. Wagner could never have seen Hoffmann's opera *Undine* (1816), and does not seem to have known the score; he would certainly have known Friedrich de la Motte Fouqué's famous story, though, and it may not be entirely a coincidence that Hoffmann's opera ends with the lovers finding union in death, in what is described as a *Liebestod*. *Undine* concerns the attempt of a water nymph to free herself of her spirit nature by finding marriage with a mortal, and was the most famous of various stories of a similar nature. The German operas of the 1820s and 1830s were filled with settings of supernatural tales by Hoffmann, Fouqué and others, as the critic Eduard Hanslick was to complain: 'Ghosts, goblins, witches, devils, earth and water spirits thronged the operatic stage […] Enthusiasm for the mysteriously demonic was kindled by *Der Freischütz* and continued to demand, like a perpetually unsatisfied need, new nourishment.'[2] This was written in connection with *Der Vampyr* (The Vampire, 1828), one of the operas by Heinrich Marschner which, together with *Hans Heiling* (1833) and *Der Templer und die Jüdin* (The Knight Templar and the Jewess, 1829), Wagner conducted and much admired.

The vampire of the opera is Lord Ruthven, a damned soul who buys extra terms of life by murdering young girls, and the plot concerns his attempts to kill three victims before midnight strikes and he must be carried off to hell. Wagner (who even composed an extra section for one of the hero Aubry's arias) would certainly have been impressed by the scene with the second of them, the pure, young village girl Emmy. Fascinated by the gruesome vampire legend, she gathers her companions round her and treats them to a ballad about a vampire:

---

2   Eduard Hanslick, '*Der Vampyr*. Romantische Oper von Heinrich Marschner', in vol. 4 of *Die Moderne Oper*, 3rd edn. (Berlin: Allgemeiner Verein
für deutsche Literatur, 1896), pp. 60–65 (author's translation).

'Sieh', Mutter, dort den bleichen Mann' ('See, Mother, over there the pale man'), she sings, and at the end of the song, there, standing before them, is the pallid figure of Ruthven. There is an inescapable connection between this and Senta's ballad, with its line 'Doch kann dem bleichen Manne Erlösung einstens noch werden' ('Yet there could be redemption one day for that pale man'), immediately after which the Dutchman stands before her. Though Wagner professed to admire *Hans Heiling* less than *Der Vampyr*, he was influenced by some of its music in the *Ring* and he would again have encountered in it the theme of the incompatibility of the human and spirit worlds, as the gloomy, brooding earth spirit Heiling attempts to break free of his subterranean kingdom of the gnomes so as to marry an innocent young village girl.

Wagner must also have admired one of Marschner's most distinctive characteristics, the treatment of principal figures in his operas as 'anti-heroes' rather than plain villains. Already in *Euryanthe* (1823), Weber had made use, in Lysiart, of a figure torn between good and evil: one of the greatest scenes in the opera reveals him struggling to assert the nobility in his nature against the darker emotions that claim him. Bois-Guilbert, in *Der Templer und die Jüdin*, has a distinct kinship to Lysiart and was admired by Wagner as 'a creature of the greatest originality of feeling'. He is a Knight Templar who attempts to abduct the heroine, Rebecca, but he has a nobler and more chivalric side which declares itself too late. Hans Heiling, though he attempts to interfere in the lives of the village folk and tries to kill his successful rival, eventually concedes defeat with some dignity, and is painted as a tragic rather than a wicked character. Even Ruthven, the vampire, makes some attempt to struggle against his nature, or the unnatural force that has possessed him, and though he is portrayed as sinister and alarming, he has a humanity that we do not meet in, say, Weber's Caspar in *Der Freischütz*.

These ambivalent characters clearly had much to offer Wagner when he was forming in his mind the mysterious figure of Vanderdecken, the Flying Dutchman. His literary sources carry little more than the seeds of such a character; and though Wagner's plot, summarized, would still suggest a ghostly visitant trying to buy his salvation at the expense of a village girl, it is evident from the Dutchman's first scene that we are in the presence of a tragic hero of larger dimensions than anything in Weber or Marschner. His emotion at Senta's obsession with him and his decision to renounce her for her own sake are moving because they arise not from some caprice of the plot, but out of a character whose stature and nobility we have come to appreciate through the music; and her final sacrifice, redeeming him with her love, is in turn true to the character of the strange, obsessed girl.

The antecedents of *Der fliegende Holländer*, however, are to be sought at least as much in *opéra comique* as in German Romantic opera. Already in the eighteenth century, French opera featured prominently in German repertories; it was to offer much to the German composers who sought the basis of a style for Romantic opera, and who rejected what they regarded as the singer-dominated trivialities of Italian opera. The resistance to Italy was more of a manifesto than a fact. In the first twenty years of the nineteenth century the influential Leipzig *Allgemeine musikalische Zeitung* carried many articles pressing the cause of French opera against Italian, but even Weber, vehement in his criticism of Italian 'Kling-Klang', wrote out of awareness of the strength of the Italian example (he had a reluctant admiration for Rossini), and Wagner, urging the value of fine singing upon the Germans, praised the Italian example and singled out Bellini for approval ('Bellini wrote melodies lovelier than one's dreams'[3]). Nevertheless, it was French *opéra comique* which provided the creative basis for German Romantic opera, in numerous ways. The increased role of the orchestra, especially to depict natural scenery and events; the development thereby made possible of the old 'reminiscence motif' into something approaching leitmotif; the tendency to move away from separate numbers into a more continuous process of development by self-contained scenes merging arioso and aria – these are but some of the characteristics that held much for German composers in general, and for Wagner in particular. From Étienne Méhul, whose work Wagner regarded as significant, and of whom,

---

3   *Cosima Wagner's Diaries*, eds. Martin Gregor-Dellin and Dietrich Mack, trans. Geoffrey Skelton, 2 vols. (London and New York: Collins, 1978–80), vol. 1, p. 519.

according to Cosima, he spoke constantly, he must have appreciated the effectiveness of allowing natural forces, including the sea, to play an integral role in the drama through the orchestra. Méhul's use of motifs must also have interested him; and it is perhaps particularly from the example of Méhul and Luigi Cherubini that there grew the ability to merge an introduction and an aria into something almost seamless (as with the Dutchman's opening 'Die Frist ist um' ['The time is up']) and, in turn, to draw such self-contained scenes into groups as the structural basis of the entire opera. It is a commonplace that the step from *Rienzi* (1842) to *Der fliegende Holländer* (1843) was one of the largest in Wagner's career; it also marks a turn from the influence of French grand opera, as cultivated by Gaspare Spontini and Daniel Auber, to that of *opéra comique*.

Not that Wagner forgot any of the lessons he learnt from Auber. He regarded *La Muette de Portici* (The Mute Girl of Portici, 1828) as the first appearance of true music drama, and the work's concentration of arias, duets and so on into a single form he particularly praised in his essay 'Erinnerungen an Auber' (Reminiscences of Auber):

> 'each of the five acts presented a drastic picture of the most extra-ordinary animation, where arias and duets in the wonted traditional sense were scarcely to be detected any more [...] the recitatives shot lightning at us; a veritable tempest whirled us onto the chorus ensembles...'[4]

He had scarcely less admiration for François-Adrien Boieldieu's most famous work, *La Dame blanche* (The White Lady, 1828), which he said had 'the finest characteristic of the French'.[5] It was an opera that held particular associations for him, as it was not only one of the first works he heard in Leipzig, but the one in which, during his time as chorus master in Würzburg, his brother Albert had made his debut as Georges Brown. His admiration for the effect of Jenny's ballad

---

4   Richard Wagner, 'Reminiscences of Auber', in *Actors and Singers*, trans. William Ashton Ellis (Lincoln and London: University of Nebraska Press, 1995), pp. 39–40.

5   *Cosima Wagner's Diaries*, vol. 1, p. 786.

was another contribution, together with Emmy's in *Der Vampyr*, to Senta's ballad and its dramatic placing; and he often expressed approval of the spinning scene – as well he might, since there is not only a comparable effect in *Der fliegende Holländer*, but even a phrase exactly cribbed. He praised the work for its 'symbolic Romanticism'.

Ironically, the grand-opera style that had won Wagner such a success with *Rienzi* in Dresden in 1842 militated against *Der fliegende Holländer* the following year. The Dresdeners, delighted with the grandiose manner of *Rienzi*, and undeterred by its enormous length, were disconcerted by what they saw as a reversion to an older, even a quainter, German Romanticism. As often with a powerfully imaginative new work, the superficies were more easily grasped than the true originality; and there were few who realized the music's real quality. Berlioz, who saw a performance, was a little reserved, impressed 'by the sombre colouring of the music and by some remarkable effects of storm and wind, which are an integral part of the dramatic character of the work'.[6] He was, however, irritated by the excess of tremolo, which he regarded as 'intellectual laziness' – a charge rare among the many that were to be levelled at Wagner's head.

How much the performance was to blame for the work's muted effect, it is hard to say. Wagner was full of praise for his admired Wilhelmine Schröder-Devrient, the singer whose dramatic power he claimed had first aroused in him the urge to compose, but very reserved about Johann Wächter as the Dutchman. Berlioz found her less impressive, complaining of 'affected poses and the spoken phrases that she finds it necessary to interject throughout the role'[7] (it must be said that other accounts of her at this stage of her career tend to support Berlioz); Wächter was, Berlioz thought, 'a really remarkable and unspoiled talent'. However, the crucial role of the orchestra remains more mysterious. The leader, Karl Lipinski, was a friend of Berlioz's, and much admired by him; Wagner was less impressed, finding Lipinski too much of a virtuoso and too wilful for the leader of what he sought – a harmonious, thoroughly blended

---

6   Hector Berlioz, *The Memoirs of Hector Berlioz*, trans. and ed. David Cairns (London: Alfred Knopf, 2002), p. 309.

7   Ibid., p. 309.

ensemble, such as his predecessor Weber had striven for. Wagner's strictures on Weber's successor Reissiger need not be taken at face value, but, for all his care for standards, Reissiger seems to have found difficulty in raising the level of the Dresden orchestra to the point at which it was really competent to deal with so demanding a score as Wagner's. Orchestrally, *Rienzi* is quite conventional beside *Der fliegende Holländer*; although the Dresden orchestra had quite a good reputation by contemporary standards, it can scarcely have been up to the demands of the new score. Berlioz reported that one of the bass players was too old even to hold up his instrument, and the lack of general discipline permitted one of the oboe players to decorate his part according to his own taste. Other accounts suggest that the resources of the Dresden house, while adequate to the general repertory and capable, it seems, of rising to the occasion of *Rienzi*, were too uneven to do full justice to *Der fliegende Holländer*. The seedy old bass player was given support by the leader of the cellos, one of the great players of his day, Friedrich Dotzauer; and Berlioz was delighted with the cor anglais player. No one dissents from the view that Wagner conducted with energy and precision. A few in the city were to sense the bold new ideas that dominated, and made something new of, all that had gone into the formation of the work; but in 1843 its day had not yet come.

An Introduction to *Der fliegende Holländer*

John Deathridge

Scots may (or may not) be pleased to hear that Wagner's *Der fliegende Holländer* was originally set in their homeland. In the manuscript score of the opera, preserved in the Bayreuth archives, the place of the action is described as 'the Scottish coast'. Senta's fiancé is a huntsman called 'Georg'. The name of her father is 'Donald', a skipper whose ship is manned by 'Scottish' sailors. The ship drops anchor in the opening scene of the opera near a coastal village with the Scottish-sounding name of 'Holystrand'. And Wagner's skipper greets the Dutchman in the third scene with the line, 'Gastfreundschaft kennt der Schotte' (literally: 'The Scotsman knows hospitality').

Two months before the Dresden premiere of *Holländer* on 2nd January 1843, Wagner changed the location of the opera from Scotland to Norway. The decision caused him a lot of work: not only did he have to go through the entire score changing the names of the characters and many of the stage directions; he also had to alter the vocal scores and many of the cues in the orchestral parts which had already been copied for the rehearsals. It is not out of the question that some of the singers actually learnt their parts *à l'écossaise*, and it is certainly not impossible that the production was being geared to show something of the wild Scottish landscape familiar to German audiences from countless plays and novels popular at the time.

Why did Wagner make the change at such a late stage? Were German opera-goers tired of Scotland? Did they prefer Scandinavian names like Sandvika and Erik (instead of Holystrand and Georg) with those striking 'k's to make them look Norwegian? Or was Wagner simply disguising his debt to Marschner and Heine? After all, Marschner's opera *Der Vampyr* also takes place in Scotland. It even has a similar constellation of characters, one of whom, like Senta's fiancé, happens to be a huntsman called Georg. Heinrich Heine, too, allows his Flying Dutchman (in the seventh chapter of his *Memoirs of Mr von Schnabelewopski*) to come ashore in Scotland where he meets a 'Scottish businessman'. And of course both Marschner and Heine knew how to exploit the typical Romantic passion for Scotland with its eerie castles, raw landscape and general air of mystery.

The most likely reason for Wagner's decision, however, is that he wanted to heighten the autobiographical significance of *Holländer*. Only a few weeks after the premiere, he published his first excursion into the art of self-profile. It was a substantial essay called 'Autobiographische Skizze' (Autobiographic Sketch, February 1843) and contained a vivid account of a hazardous voyage along the Norwegian coastline which Wagner had undertaken on his way to Paris shortly before beginning work on *Holländer*. What could have been more effective than to give the opera a similar atmosphere? 'The passage through the Norwegian reefs,' Wagner wrote, 'made a wonderful impression on my imagination; the legend of the Flying Dutchman, which the sailors verified, took on a distinctive, strange colouring that only my sea adventures could have given it.'[1]

* * *

If the idea of moving *Holländer* from Scotland to Norway was one of the young Wagner's most brilliant autobiographical *coups de théâtre*, it is not surprising that the mature Wagner reinterpreted the opera to make it conform to his later theories. His ingenuity in creating an apparent unity between (German) art and (German) life was matched only by his equally ingenious attempts to see his early works, particularly *Holländer*, as precursors of the music drama.

---

1   Richard Wagner, 'Autobiographic Sketch', *Richard Wagner's Prose Works*, trans. William Ashton Ellis, 8 vols. (London: Kegan Paul, Trench, Trübner & Co., 1892–99; Lincoln and London: University of Nebraska Press, 1995), vol. 1, pp. 13–14 (trans. modified).

One of the most famous and influential passages in this vein comes from his essay 'Eine Mitteilung an meine Freunde' (A Communication to My Friends, 1851) which was written while he was at work on the libretto of the *Ring*:

> I remember, before I set about the actual working-out of *Der fliegende Holländer*, to have first drafted Senta's Ballad in the second act, and completed both its verse and melody. In this piece, I unconsciously laid the thematic germ of the whole music of the opera... In the eventual composition of the music, the thematic picture that had come alive within me spread itself, as if of its own accord, as an integrated network over the entire drama.[2]

Senta's Ballad is certainly dramatically central to *Holländer*. But no impartial listener could describe it as the musical plasma from which the rest of the opera grew. Nor could he or she hear its themes as 'an integrated network' cast 'over the entire drama' without an exceptional leap of acoustic faith. Wagner is being tendentious, too, when he suggests that Senta's Ballad was the first number to be composed. What he does not say is that, before writing the libretto of *Holländer* in 1841, he wrote three songs from the opera for a Paris audition in the previous year: Senta's Ballad, the Norwegian sailors' song in Act Three, 'Steuermann, lass die Wacht' ('Steersman, leave your watch') and the so-called Phantom Song, or *Spukgesang*, sung by the Dutchman's crew in the same scene. Any one of these pieces could have had musical priority. All three were composed at the same time and were obviously intended as operatic 'numbers' in the traditional sense. As we shall see, their musical and dramatic significance was by no means limited to Senta's Ballad.

The supreme irony of Wagner's later interpretation is that he overlooked the virtues of his own music. Like many writers who have taken his words at face value, he came to believe that *Holländer* was a closely integrated network of organically related themes. In fact, the opera tends to go in the opposite direction. What makes it so ef-

---

2   Richard Wagner, 'A Communication to My Friends', *Richard Wagner's Prose Works* (see footnote 1) vol. 1, p. 370 (trans. modified).

fective is not the sophisticated leitmotif system of, say, the *Ring*, but a rumbustious ragbag of disparate elements that sounds quite unlike the seamless textures of the mature music dramas. *Holländer* is full of violent contrasts, grisly orchestration,[3] simple tunes, huge leaps from one style to another, and a host of stock techniques used with originality and panache. Although Wagner does make use of the so-called 'reminiscence motif' (the recall of telling musical phrases associated with specific moods or characters), his application of it in the opera is sporadic and without the subtle complexity of his later music.

The real musical and dramatic crux of *Holländer* is the verse song. Two of Wagner's later works, *Tannhäuser* (1845) and *Die Meistersinger von Nürnberg* (1868), are famous examples of the use of song (i.e. the actual act of singing) as a dramatic symbol or metaphor. The Song to Venus, sung by the protagonist in *Tannhäuser*, and Walther's Prize Song in *Die Meistersinger* both have extra-musical ambitions that are meant to convey the idealism of the artist or the glories of German Art. And Wagner cleverly distinguishes between the song as a dramatic object and the 'normal' singing that surrounds it by using a realistic frame: the organization of a formal competition or 'War of Song' (*Sängerkrieg*) in *Tannhäuser*, and Walther's 'lesson' with Hans Sachs in *Die Meistersinger* in which he learns how to shape the Prize Song according to the rules of true art.

Wagner's use of song in *Holländer* is hardly less important. Although at first sight without any conspicuous cultural message,[4]

---

3   Especially in its use of the wind instruments, the orchestration of *Holländer* shows the unmistakable influence of Berlioz and Mendelssohn – two composers whom the mature Wagner regarded publicly with unpleasant condescension. Wagner admitted privately to the London critic Eduard Dannreuther that he had made a 'detailed study' of Berlioz's orchestration in *Roméo et Juliette* as early as 1840, the year in which he composed the three numbers from *Holländer* for a Paris audition. He later presented Berlioz with a copy of the first edition of *Tristan und Isolde* which is now in the Bibliothèque Nationale in Paris. The dedication reads: 'To the great and esteemed composer of *Roméo et Juliette*'.

4   At second sight, after a careful look at Wagner's public statements during the composition of *Holländer* in Paris, any reader aware of his constant political attitude towards music and opera here (and later) can hardly fail to detect his intention to depict the supposedly indigenous songs in the

his treatment of the song forms in the opera ingeniously expresses the tension between normality and mystery central to the work. There are five songs in all: the Steersman's song in Act One; the Spinning Chorus and Senta's Ballad in Act Two; and the two songs of the Norwegian sailors and the Dutchman's crew in Act Three. What sets them apart as songs in the literal sense, as opposed to the 'normal' singing that makes up the rest of the opera, is that they are inevitably interrupted by a real event. Indeed, the unfinished songs of *Holländer* could be seen as a striking, and uncannily precise metaphor for the frustrated passion of the protagonist. The Steersman falls asleep like the Dormouse in *Alice in Wonderland*. Senta breaks off the spinning chorus by telling it to 'stop that stupid song' (a remark that delighted Wagner's critics). The song of the Norwegian sailors is interrupted by *another* song, the Phantom Song of the Dutchman's crew. And Senta leaves her Ballad unfinished by breaking off the third refrain with a text of her own in the first person: 'Ich sei's, die dich durch ihre Treu' erlöse! / Mög' Gottes Engel mich dir zeigen! / Durch mich sollst du das Heil erreichen!' ('Let me be the one whose loyalty shall save you! / May God's angel reveal me to you! / Through me shall you attain redemption!').

* * *

OVERTURE

The *Holländer* Overture is the best proof (if any were needed) that the songs of the opera are central to its musical conception. Although it was written last, in the later summer of 1841, the Overture con-

---

opera as a primal scene of 'healthy' German music in opposition to the 'decadence' of French (and Italian) opera. The last-minute translation of the location of *Holländer* from Scotland, familiar to respectable *bürgerlich* readers of Walter Scott throughout Europe, to the less familiar northern clime of Norway can also be seen as an attempt by Wagner to transform the locale into an even more northerly 'north' and, hence, a more purely anti-French and anti-Enlightenment place than he had at first envisaged. See John Deathridge, *Wagner beyond Good and Evil* (Berkeley, Los Angeles, London: University of California Press, 2008), pp. 29–30.

sists mainly of ideas drawn from the three songs set to music for the Paris audition in 1840 which were the first sections of the work to be composed.[5]

The first group of themes is taken from the Phantom Song of the Dutchman's crew [1, 2, 3].[6] Like that song, the music launches almost at once into a series of giddy movements that quickly obscure the opening key. After a short time in which a lot seems to happen, we hear a virile theme taken from the Dutchman's monologue in Act One [4] which soon subsides into the gentle refrain of Senta's Ballad [5]. Wagner never tired of comparing these 'masculine' and 'feminine' elements in the opera with Faust and Gretchen in Goethe's famous play. The idea, of course, is really an astonishing piece of musical cunning. The shock of the opening heightens the plaintive melody of the Ballad: having dazzled our ears with violent sounds, Wagner beguiles them with the sweet and sentimental. The stylistic contrast could not be greater. Nor could it sum up the vigorous emotion of the whole opera to better effect.

The rest of the Overture is a pot-pourri of themes and sounds from the Norwegian sailors' song [10, 11], Senta's Ballad [5, 8] and the wild cries of the Dutchman's crew [2, 7], bound together by snatches from the Dutchman's monologue [4, 6, 9]. Wagner concludes with yet another brilliant stroke that is the essence of the opera. Instead of finishing with one of the songs, as we might expect, he builds the conclusion around the theme which Senta sings when she *interrupts* her Ballad [12]. It is as if the upward rush of the violins that introduces the final section were to wrench the Overture from the conditional into the present tense. The change of key from D minor to D major, too, creates a mood of affirmation – the transformation of a remote world into a physical reality.

---

5   Another sign that the Overture was in Wagner's mind at an early stage is the resemblance between its opening and the beginning of Beethoven's Ninth Symphony. According to Wagner's own accounts, this work made a profound impression on him during the first months of his Paris sojourn. It therefore seems likely that he deliberately converted the mysterious bare fifths of Beethoven's opening into the rasping sound of the open fifths at the beginning of *Holländer* overture – the 'salty breeze' which Franz Liszt claimed to hear in the piece.

6   Numbers in square brackets refer to the Thematic Guide on pp. 73–77 [Ed.].

Example 1:
The opening bars of Beethoven's Ninth Symphony (above) and the *Der fliegende Holländer* Overture (below). See footnote 5.

ACT ONE

No. 1 Introduction

Because so many good things happen later in *Holländer*, the mastery of its opening scene has often been overlooked. The scene is built around the cries of the Norwegian sailors [13, 14] and the Steersman's song. Between these colourful figures, Wagner inserted the prosaic figure of Daland (Senta's father) who sings some appropriately four-square music. Ernest Newman once criticized Wagner for giving Daland some monotonous melodies, including his first arioso [16]. But Newman gave little credit to Wagner's dramatic instinct. Daland's music may be sometimes dull when seen in isolation, but in the context of the Sailors' and the Steersman's songs, not to mention the whistling of the wind expressed by a short figure played by the piccolo [15], the effect is exactly right. Daland is the epitome of normality. Why shouldn't his music be unexceptional too?

The centre point of the scene is the Steersman's song. It is introduced by a wide-leaping tune [17], alternating with the rushing of the violas and cellos. We can already sense what is going to happen:

the Steersman is fighting his tiredness and the waves are beginning to move in anticipation of the Dutchman's arrival. The song is built around two memorable themes [18, 19] and its first verse concludes with a violent movement of the waves portrayed by thumping timpani and strings alternating with jagged wind chords. Once Wagner has imprinted the full context of the song on our ears, he uses it a second time to create a specific effect. The technique is as simple as it is ingenious. All Wagner does is to space out the phrases of the second verse so that the gaps become longer and longer. Thus he not only gives us a musical description of how the Steersman falls asleep, but also fills the ever-widening spaces with disturbing sounds which vividly portray the arrival of the Dutchman's ship. By the time the Steersman loses control of his tiredness, the last fragment of his song has vanished and the Dutchman steps ashore.

No. 2 Aria

The Dutchman's monologue begins with a grinding figure in the violas and cellos which expresses his desperate mood exactly [20]. Wagner was a master of concision. If you don't believe this, just listen carefully to this opening. Note how Wagner builds the phrase around the interval of the diminished fifth or tritone E sharp/B, which is echoed by the horn in the second bar. What could be a more precise musical description of the Dutchman's demonic aura? And if you are puzzled by the term 'diminished fifth', you may be interested to know that it is an interval which medieval theorists referred to as the 'Devil in Music' (*Diabolus in Musica*). Even in the Romantic Age, it never quite lost its bad reputation.

The opening recitative of the monologue builds in intensity until it tumbles into a long aria. In contrast to the 'organic' view of the *Holländer* music encouraged by the mature Wagner, the three main themes of the aria have little to do with one another [21, 22, 23]. In fact, the music thrives on the abrupt changes and manic repetitions that propel it forward. There is little formal repetition; and when it does occur, it only serves to confirm the sense of endless chaos. The intensity of the aria seems futile because its thematic disunity is really what holds it together. And once again Wagner beautifully summarizes this dramatic and musical paradox with a remote and spine-chilling vignette. As the monologue draws to its close, the music moves unexpectedly from C minor into the distant key of E minor. The Dutchman's crew sings the short but telling phrase 'Ew'ge Vernichtung, nimm uns auf' ('Eternal extinction, fall on us'), and the music, just as unexpectedly, returns quickly to C minor. It is a fleeting touch that exactly mirrors the aria's disruptive mood.

No. 3 *Scene, Duet and Chorus*

Daland wakes his sleepy Steersman who sings another snatch from the second verse of his song. At the end of the scene the Norwegian sailors add another verse to the same song. Thus the whole scene and the entire first act appear to be in a surrounding frame consisting of the Steersman's song. The events of the present scene (and the preceding monologue of the Dutchman) are in parenthesis, so to speak, between the second and third verses.

When Daland eventually notices the Dutchman, Wagner introduces a crawling phrase on the lower strings [24]. Again, it is a precise musical description of what is happening: the Dutchman is seeking shelter and wants to persuade Daland to give it to him. The phrase is recalled again and again as the Dutchman gives Daland a self-pitying account of his fateful journeys. Its inevitable return to the same upper note is a painful negation that expresses the vicious circle in which the Dutchman finds himself. The following duet, too, is a good example of Wagner's knack of finding suitable musical metaphors to reflect specific situations. The Dutchman sings in long cantilenas while Daland gloats over the possibility of doing business with him in short snappy phrases reminiscent of French comic opera. When Daland reveals that he has a daughter he could offer to the Dutchman, his words are introduced with a short phrase [25] that is a glaring contrast to the pessimism of the Dutchman's music. It may not be one of Wagner's most 'inspired' musical ideas; but its sharp rhythm and regular upward movement could be seen as a clever stylistic symbol of Daland's banal optimism.

Transition

At the end of Act One the Norwegian sailors raise the anchor of their ship and hoist the sails. According to Wagner's directions the scene must then change as quickly as possible. The musical transition mirrors the transformation ingeniously with a lilting two-note motif taken from the song of the Norwegian sailors [14] that literally weaves its way into the Spinning Song [26] at the beginning of Act Two. Wagner has made it clear in the Overture that this motif is derived from a single bar in Senta's Ballad (compare [5a] fourth bar, [8], [14] and [26]). Thus within the short space of the transition he spins a thematic thread that connects together three songs central to the opera, two of which appear in the following scene. This is not part of the mythical network of themes he later claimed to have cast 'over the entire drama'. It is rather that the songs form a group which, precisely because of its inner connectedness, stands out in sharp relief against the rest of the work. Wagner is matching single pieces of dramatic and musical clothing, not an entire wardrobe.

ACT TWO

No. 4 Song, Scene, Ballad and Chorus

The breezy A major of the Spinning Song [26] that opens this scene is intended as a direct contrast with, and at the same time a formal parallel to, the minor key of Senta's Ballad [27] that follows it. The Ballad is usually sung in G minor. In Wagner's manuscript score, however, it is in A minor; and although the link with the Spinning Song is hardly impaired by the transposition, the apposition of A major and A minor in the original version is clearly significant.

Many composers from Mozart and Schubert to Mahler were fond of blending a major chord or key into a minor one with the same root. You can try out the effect on the piano by playing a simple chord of A major followed immediately by A minor. The contrast of mood could not be greater or more simply achieved. Indeed,

Wagner was to base large sections of a later work, *Lohengrin*, on exactly the same effect. In the original version of *Holländer*, too, the light-hearted A major of the Spinning Song is gradually merged into the melancholy A minor of Senta's Ballad. Both songs have three verses and are interrupted by Senta for profoundly different reasons. Thus a larger form emerges that embraces both pieces and the entire scene too. Wagner completes the form by returning to A major for the final chorus. The tune is jolly and deliberately superficial [28] – another almost devilish imitation of French *opéra comique*. Its hysterical mood is appropriate: after the magic of Senta's Ballad the 'normal' world of everyday routine is never quite the same again.

No. 5 *Duet*

The centre-point of the duet between Senta and Erik is the so-called Dream Narration. Although *Holländer* is hardly a fledgling music drama, as the mature Wagner tended to think, this scene is certainly a premonition of his later interest (via the philosopher Arthur Schopenhauer) in dreams and the unconscious. Indeed, soon after the first performance he added a suggestive stage direction to the duet that implies at least a passing acquaintance with the ideas of Franz Mesmer and the Marquis de Puységur – two early pioneers in the discovery of the unconscious, whose work greatly interested the German Romantics.[7] The direction reads: 'At the beginning of Erik's narration she sinks into a magnetic sleep, so

---

7   Readers interested in the history of psychoanalysis may like to know that *Der fliegende Holländer* was one of Wagner's works that attracted the attention of Freud's circle in Vienna during its early years. The small group that met regularly in Freud's house to discuss his ideas admittedly concentrated more on the biographical significance of *Holländer* than on its contribution to the theory of dreams. Nevertheless, a paper entitled 'Richard Wagner in *Der fliegende Holländer*' read to the circle by Max Graf casts new light on the character of Erik (who does not appear in Heine's account of the story) and Wagner's reasons for inventing him. See vol. 9 of *Schriften zur angewandten Seelenkunde*, ed. Siegmund Freud (Leipzig and Vienna: Deuticke, 1911–25).

that she appears to be dreaming the dream being related to her.' The significance of this is that Wagner created the dramatic situation before he rationalized it. In the original manuscript score we read simply that 'Senta approaches Erik'. But the text and the music already suggest that Senta is mesmerized by Erik's vision. The new direction is merely a more telling visual realization of the composer's aural imagination. Like the Dream Narration itself, Wagner's fantasy was ahead of reality.

Wagner prepares the Dream Narration with characteristic skill. The hapless Erik is bursting to tell Senta of his woes. Appropriately, Wagner gives him a short-breathed melody [29] that refuses to unfold – actually a technical shortcoming which he turned to precise dramatic advantage. The very awkwardness of Erik's music is astonishingly effective. Its broken structure is not only a reflection of his lack of skill in expressing himself, it is also a stubborn contrast to the taut continuous texture of the following narration.

In an irrational outburst, Erik accuses Senta of being ensnared by Satan, and almost the entire orchestra answers his diminished fifth (the 'Devil in Music') with a frenetic repetition of a single chord [30]. The Dream Narration begins. Senta listens spellbound to Erik, recreating each detail of his dream of how her father brings a mysterious stranger to the house. But when Erik relates his vision of her fleeing with the stranger across the ocean, she awakens abruptly. Her 'magnetic sleep' is interrupted by the realistic thought that *she* is the woman the stranger is looking for. Senta retreats into her imagination once more and sings the remaining few bars of the Ballad omitted in the previous scene [5b]. Even this fragment is left incomplete: instead of singing the final note she utters a cry of fright as her father enters with the Dutchman. Erik's dream is now a reality.

No. 6 Finale – Aria, Duet and Trio

If Senta's Ballad and Erik's Dream Narration tell exciting stories about the Dutchman which are full of adventure and euphoric detail, his actual presence on the stage is surprisingly sober. He enters to the accompaniment of the timpani alone [31] – one of those ominous pulsations that Wagner never tired of using to create low-key tension. He is followed by Daland who sings a business-as-usual aria based on a pretty melody with a distinct flavour of Berlioz [32]. Characteristically, Wagner never develops the tune with the suavity it deserves. The music keeps stopping and starting as if something were amiss with Daland's calculations. And, as usual, Wagner's aural instincts are right: Senta is attracted to the Dutchman as Daland anticipated, but there is a tension between them he does not understand. Surprised and perplexed, he leaves.

For singers and listeners alike, the following duet between Senta and the Dutchman is one of the most exhausting numbers in the opera. Although full of Italianate melody and French-like orchestration, it sounds heavy-handed. Even the verve of the concluding theme [33] fails to enliven the Dutchman's laboured advances and Senta's righteous avowal of faith unto death. Only the return of Senta's father saves the situation. In an influential introduction to *Holländer*, Liszt wrote that he regretted Wagner's undercutting of the passionate thrust of the music with the prosaic reappearance of Daland. Liszt misunderstood Wagner's dramatic strategy: if the second act had ended with a love duet, the tension between fantasy and reality central to the opera would have been weakened. Daland interrupts the duet with a march-like theme [34] that brings us down to earth with a jolt. The 'ideal' world of Senta and the Dutchman is never quite the same again.

Transition

The scene changes from a room in Daland's house to the bay outside where the ship of the Norwegians, full of life and bright festivity, is seen alongside the sinister darkness of the Dutchman's vessel. The transition is built mainly from the introductory tune to the Steersman's song [17] and snatches from the song of the Norwegian sailors [10, 11, 14] that opens the third act.

ACT THREE

No. 7 *Chorus and Ensemble*

From a structural and orchestral point of view, this scene is one of the most inventive in the opera. Wagner's virtuosity in combining and distending various sounds to portray the growing excitement of the Norwegians as they try to goad some life out of the Dutchman's crew is without precedent in his early works. His use of song, too, is even more ingenious than in previous scenes.

The Norwegian sailors sing three verses of their song. After the first verse there is a merry interlude during which the Sailors and their girlfriends taunt the Dutchman's crew. Wagner throws a musical shadow of unease over the festivities with the introductory tune of the Steersman's song in the minor key [35], some harmonic effects [36] and the transformation of a motif from the Phantom Song of the Dutchman's crew into another diminished fifth, or 'Devil in Music' [37]. By the time the sailors sing the second verse of their song, the mysterious ship is beginning to show signs of movement. The jittery orchestration betrays the growing fear of the Norwegians, whose song in C major is now interrupted by the Phantom Song of the Dutchman's crew in the remote key of B minor. The ghostly sailors sing two fearsome verses. And Wagner's crowning act of musical and theatrical mastery arrives when he combines the third verses of both songs in two different and remotely related keys. The Norwegians are reduced to silence by the wild apparition; and with a loud cry of raucous laughter the Phantom Song of the Dutchman's crew disintegrates.

No. 8 *Duet, Cavatina and Finale*

Erik enters with Senta in great agitation. In an impassioned duet he implores her in vain not to uphold her vow of eternal fidelity to the Dutchman. The vicious circle in which Erik and Senta are entwined is reflected by two motifs [38, 39] that are repeated incessantly without development. Like the short phrase used to express the Dutchman's futile existence in his first confrontation with Daland in Act One [24], both figures have a tendency to negate themselves by returning to the same upper note. The music creates an atmosphere of hopelessness and impending disaster. Even the simple honesty of Erik's cavatina [40] cannot change Senta's decision. Her bond with the Dutchman is inviolable.

When the Dutchman sees and overhears Erik and Senta together, he immediately assumes that Senta has been unfaithful to him. Deeply disappointed, he boards the ship and departs. Nevertheless, Senta's bond with him and the sinister world he represents is unshaken. While Senta's counterpart in Marschner's opera *Der Vampyr* marries her middle-class fiancé after breaking with the demonic forces that have enticed her, Senta remains true to her vow of eternal fidelity to the Dutchman by committing suicide. Wagner borrowed the idea from Heine who pointed out the moral of the tale with exquisite irony: 'Women must be careful of [...] marrying a Flying Dutchman; and we men can see from the piece how, in the best of circumstances, women are the ruin of us all.'[8] But Wagner preferred a less conventional and more ambiguous ending. Senta and Erik are neither drawn closer together by their escapade with the supernatural, nor is the redemption of the Dutchman by Senta's suicide framed by sceptical common sense. Wagner combines the typical happy end of romantic opera with the tragic conclusion of French grand opera, and to do this he had to reject both Heine's seemingly amoral wit and Marschner's bland respectability. The Dutchman is freed from the curse upon him and Senta from her petty existence among small-minded spinners and worthy huntsmen. But Senta's relationship with Erik is destroyed, and her family and friends are left in disarray. As the Dutchman rises 'transfigured' above the ocean with Senta in his arms, Wagner's music makes it easy to forget that the demonic has triumphed.

* * *

---

8   Heinrich Heine, 'Aus den Memoiren des Herrn Schnabelewopski', *Historisch-kritische Gesamtausgabe der Werke*, ed. Manfred Windfuhr, vol. 5 (Hamburg: Hoffmann und Campe, 1994), p. 174.

When Wagner moved the setting of *Der fliegende Holländer* from Scotland to Norway, it was only the first of many alterations he made to the work. For the first performances he transposed Senta's Ballad into G minor and relinquished the idea of playing the three acts of the opera without an interval. He undertook major revisions of the orchestration in 1846, and again in 1852 when he retouched the instrumentation of the ending of the Overture. For a performance in Weimar in 1853, he expressly asked Liszt, who was to conduct the opera, to change the orchestration of a single chord: the accompaniment of Senta's cry at the beginning of the second act Finale. For his Paris concerts in 1860, he made two major additions to the ending of the Overture and added a harp to its orchestration. He even began a completely new version of Senta's Ballad (a sketch of which has survived) for a model performance of *Holländer* in Munich for King Ludwig II of Bavaria, who had, since 1864, become Wagner's patron. In the 1870s too, he told his publishers that he intended to revise the opera further before having the full score engraved. Cosima's diaries report on 9th April 1880 that Wagner 'wants to postpone the dictation of the autobiography until after the performance of *Parsifal*, when he also wants to [...] rearrange *Der fliegende Holländer*'.[9] And as late as 8th September 1881, just a year and a half before Wagner's death, Cosima writes: 'At teatime Richard talks about *Der fliegende Holländer* and tells me that it makes him sad to find in it so much noisiness and so many repetitions that damage the work.'[10]

Wagner was preoccupied at regular intervals with *Holländer* for a major part of his life. Although he never found time to give posterity a final 'definitive' version, it is perhaps possible to deduce something of what he had in mind from his revision of the ending of the Overture in 1860. The ending (like the ending of the whole opera) is built around the theme that Senta sings when she interrupts her Ballad [12]. For his Paris concerts, Wagner added twenty-one bars in the style of *Tristan und Isolde* and allowed the refrain of the Ballad [5] to sound once more in the concluding bars. Not only the music, but

9   *Cosima Wagner's Diaries*, vol. 2, p. 464 (trans. modified).
10 Ibid., p. 717 (trans. modified).

also its dramatic point was therefore given a new flavour. Instead of remaining outside the Ballad in the triumphant-sounding key of D major, the new ending takes a leap backwards into the meditative atmosphere of the song with chromatic modulations, the evocative sound of the harp, and the final quotation from the Ballad itself. This version, which is usually the one that is played today, assumes a more introspective character that smooths over the raw vitality of the original. Why did Wagner make the change? Did he, like Senta, want to turn fantasy into reality by recomposing the music to make it fit his later interpretation of *Holländer* as a potential music drama? Or did he simply want to improve the opera's lack of technical sophistication? We shall never know. But the hybrid style of the revisions he did make at least tend to show that the work is not the inherently German precursor of the music drama that Wagner wanted posterity to think it was. Despite his attempts to change it, *Der fliegende Holländer* has stubbornly remained a vigorous and refreshingly cosmopolitan opera that was originally conceived for Paris, first performed in Germany, influenced by French, German and Italian music – and originally set in Scotland.

Loneliness, Love and Death

William Vaughan

> *The form of* Der fliegende Holländer *is the mythical poem
> of the folk: a primeval trait of man's essential nature is
> expressed here with overwhelming power. This trait, in its
> widest sense, is the longing for peace from life's storms.*
>
> Richard Wagner[1]

It is usually in their early works that artists reveal their roots most
clearly. *Der fliegende Holländer* is no exception. The theme, even
more than the music, is steeped in the cultural preoccupations of
the early nineteenth century. To some extent this was deliberate. At
the time Wagner was desperately seeking to establish his reputation
and undoubtedly he chose the subject with an eye to its popular
appeal. But this is only half the story. Wagner was, as well, genuinely
fascinated by the implications of the legend, and identified strongly
with them.

The legend had already attracted considerable attention before
Wagner chose it for his opera. He based his libretto on the version
that had appeared in the poet Heinrich Heine's *Salon* in 1834. The
story had first appeared in print in 1821 in *Blackwood's Magazine*,
and many forms of it were subsequently published in France, Eng-
land and Germany.

The legend itself is older. The figure of Vanderdecken as such – the
Dutchman in Spanish Costume – suggests a date in the seventeenth

---

1 'The Art-work of the Future' in *Richard Wagner's Prose Works*, trans. and
ed. William Ashton Ellis (London: Kegan Paul, Trench, Trübner & Co.,
1892–99) vol. 1, p. 306.

century. The folklorist Rolf Engert has, however, pointed out features which would indicate that this is just an adaptation of a theme of greater antiquity.[2] The fatal oath sworn by the Dutchman – to round the Cape of Good Hope even if this should take him to the Day of Judgement – is similar to one said to have been made by the great Portuguese explorer Vasco da Gama in 1498 when he rounded the Cape for the first time. The fear of the ordinary sailor at the intrepid nature of da Gama and other Renaissance explorers may well have inspired the original legend. But it may go back further even than this, to a much earlier group of seamen adventurers – the Vikings.

The interest in recording and elaborating it in the early nineteenth century reflects the then-current vogue for folk tales; a vogue which we must thank for having stimulated many magnificent collections, including the works of the Brothers Grimm. In Germany, folk literature had taken on particular significance. Already in the middle of the previous century the writer J.G. Herder had emphasized how it enshrined the imaginative power and closeness to nature of primitive peoples. Later writers – notably the poet Novalis – were fascinated by the way in which the fantasy of the folk tale embodied levels of experience normally closed to more rational discourse. With their great interest in reviving national culture, many German Romantic artists had drawn upon both the forms and the themes of folk literature, and Wagner inherited this concern for the national and psychological dimensions of myth. In the case of the 'mythical poem' of *Der fliegende Holländer*, it is the psychological, rather than the national, that predominates.

Even before it was written down, the Flying Dutchman legend had made its impact on literature. For English readers the most notable instance is Coleridge's *The Rime of the Ancient Mariner* (1798). Although Coleridge's poem is far from a simple reworking of the legend, it shares the central theme of a sailor condemned to continuous wandering for a blasphemy. There may also be a specific reference to the Dutchman legend in the description of the death ship that appears after the Mariner has shot the albatross, and he and his

---

2   Rolf Engert, *Die Sage vom Fliegenden Holländer* (Berlin: Mittler & Sohn, 1927).

comrades are stricken with thirst. For, in the traditional version of the legend, the Dutchman's ship brings death or misfortune to those who encounter her.

As John Livingston Lowes suggested in *The Road to Xanadu*,[3] Coleridge presumably came across the legend amongst the sea folk of the West Country where he was living at the time. But, like Wagner, he appears to have been encouraged to rework it by the example of German poets. Like Goethe, Schiller and Gottfried Bürger, he aimed to emulate the simple rhythmic structure of folk ballads, and shared their interest in developing the fantasy and emotional elements in the traditional stories. In the case of the Dutchman this was to lead to an important shift of emphasis. In the legend the Dutchman is no hero, but a warning against the consequences of breaking the natural law. In the Romantic treatments of the theme, by contrast, he is viewed with sympathy. The painfulness of his punishment is dwelt upon, and the possibility of his salvation is entertained.

A similar change can be found at the time in the attitude to other traditional stories where the protagonist defies the will of God. In all there is a fascination with the fate of the protagonist, with the way he moved beyond normal experience, often wandering through vast dimensions of space or time. The quest for limitless experience seemed to take on a justification of its own. The most celebrated of these legends were, of course, Faust – the scholar who sold his soul to the Devil for a share of supernatural power – and Don Juan – the libertine who would stop at nothing in his pursuit of the erotic. These works were in everyone's minds at the time, having formed the basis of masterpieces by Goethe, Mozart and Byron. Goethe's *Faust* was particularly in Wagner's mind when he was composing his opera, and he had, in fact, just completed a *Faust* overture that presages the musical style of the *Holländer*. The concept of Vanderdecken's release from his curse through the faithful love of Senta obviously parallels the conclusion of Goethe's play, where Faust is redeemed through the intercession of Gretchen. The idea that the Dutchman was saved through the love of a woman had been an innovation

---

3   John Livingston Lowes, *The Road to Xanadu: A Study in the Ways of the Imagination* (Boston: Houghton Mifflin, 1927).

of Heine's which may have been intended as a deliberate satire on Goethe's work. Be that as it may, the innovation was seized upon by Wagner and developed with eagerness.

Faust, Don Juan and the Flying Dutchman appealed to the Romantics as rebels. Of the three, however, the Dutchman is the only one whose punishment – rather than crime – forms the focus of the story. Where Faust and Don Juan wander at will, in a constant search for new adventure, the Dutchman wanders only because he is seeking the peace of death. Even the addition of the notion of his salvation through the love of a woman does not detract from the isolation and emptiness of his meanderings across the ocean.

The loneliness of the Dutchman is at the heart of the legend. Rolf Engert has suggested that this expresses the basic predicament of the sailor, who sails in order to reach land, but has no purpose when he gets there but to set out to sea again. This certainly explains why it developed so powerfully amongst sailors – particularly among those of northern Europe who had become accustomed to undertaking voyages of long duration. When the legend was taken up by the Romantics this loneliness took on new dimensions. In an age when the artist came increasingly to see his role as that of the outsider, independent of conventional society, it seemed that he must neces- sarily suffer the burden of isolation as payment for the originality of his vision. *'L'indépendance a pour consequence l'isolement'* ('In- dependence leads to isolation'), wrote the French author Benjamin Constant in his autobiographical novel *Adolphe* (1816).

The image of the artist as a lonely wanderer occurs frequently in Romantic art and literature. It can be seen, for example, in one of the most celebrated German paintings of the time, Caspar David Fried- rich's *Monk by the Sea* (1809), where the artist has portrayed himself wandering alone, sunk in contemplation, in an endless, featureless waste. 'It is delicious', wrote the author Clemens Brentano on seeing this picture in 1810, 'to experience an infinite solitude at the edge of the sea beneath a murky sky, to cast one's gaze out over a limitless waste of water. It is something else again to have made the voyage there and back, instead of which one wishes to pass over to the other side and cannot; one is stripped of everything necessary for life and yet perceives the voice of that life in the rumbling of the waves, the sighing of the air, the passage of clouds, the solitary cry of birds.'[4]

Heine introduces the Dutchman as 'the Wandering Jew of the ocean', a reference to another popular legend. Ahasuerus, like Vanderdecken, was doomed for blasphemy to ceaseless wandering, until the Day of Judgement. His crime was to have taunted Jesus on the way to Calvary. Coleridge merged the two legends in condemning his Mariner to wander on both land and sea; Goethe and Shelley were among writers later to be attracted by the theme. Ludovic Halévy's grand opera *Le Juif errant* (The Wandering Jew, 1852) sets the legendary figure in a historical (medieval) context and concludes with a celestial vision of the Court of Heaven, before the Angel of Death orders the hapless Jew to continue – '*Marche! Marche toujours!*' Indeed, the Wandering Jew continued to be used as a metaphor for the artist for a long time, often by surprising people, such as the French Realist painter Gustave Courbet. His portrait of himself with a patron, *Bonjour, Monsieur Courbet* (1854), is based upon a popular print of the Wandering Jew. But then Courbet, Realist though he was, had an ego as big as that of any Romantic artist.

The isolation of the Dutchman, reinforced by that of the Wandering Jew, had strong personal associations for both Heine and Wagner. Not only were they both, as artists, metaphorical exiles. They were also literal exiles, Germans living in Paris. The very different characters of their exiles are reflected in their attitudes to the Dutchman theme. Heine had left Germany in 1831, finding the atmosphere uncongenial to his liberal sympathies, and there was little to encourage him to return. Indeed, his writings were branded in 1835 as politically subversive. Artistically, too, he had distanced himself, for he was one of those artists who were trying to free themselves from Romantic attitudes that seemed outworn. He treated the dominant themes of the day with irony.

---

4   *Berliner Abendblätter,* No. 12, 13th October 1810. See S. Hinz (ed.) *Caspar David Friedrich in Briefe und Bekenntnissen* (Berlin: Henschelverlag, 1968), p. 222.

This sense of distancing and irony can be found in Heine's account of the Dutchman legend. He pretends that his narrator saw it performed as a play in Amsterdam. He embroiders the theme by adding the Romantic notion of the Dutchman being redeemable through the faithful love of a woman. Then he makes light of it. 'The Devil, fool that he is, doesn't believe in the faithfulness of women.' The whole play simply becomes a frame for the most fickle of encounters with a Dutch adventuress that his narrator comes across in the audience.

Salvation, for Heine, is not to be taken seriously. For Wagner it was a different matter. All irony is removed in his adaptation of Heine's narrative. He may have been an exile at the time, but he had every hope of being redeemed through the establishment of a brilliant career. Yet even in his vision of redemption Wagner is aware of the peculiar position of the artist. The Dutchman does not return to earthly existence. And Wagner the artist, in his moment of triumph, would not re-enter the bourgeois world.

In a sense, Wagner was reclaiming Heine's version of the legend for Romanticism. For while this tendency had all but run its course in literature, it was still a potent force in music. Indeed, Wagner could be seen as the culmination of the movement in Germany, a view that would accord well with the assertion by A.W. Schlegel and other Romantic theorists that music was the supreme art form. The seriousness with which Wagner viewed the story can be seen in the way that he handled its details. He is deeply aware of its basis in folklore. It seems significant that he should have shown Senta in a dreamlike state when we first encounter her. She is musing before the Dutchman's portrait. The legendary enters her life, so to speak, through the state of dreaming. Nothing could have been more typical of the German Romantic attitude to folk tales. Like dreams, they were seen as a means of access to the dark, unconscious side of experience. The two were specifically linked by Novalis when he claimed, 'All fabulous tales are no more than dreams of that native world that is everywhere and nowhere'.[5] He himself used the notion of the dream

5   As cited by Carlyle in 'Novalis', *Foreign Review*, 1829. See Thomas Carlyle, *Critical and Miscellaneous Writings*, (London: Chapman and Hall, 1839), vol. 1, p. 181.

entering conscious life in his novel *Heinrich von Ofterdingen*, where the hero's dream of a mystical blue flower at the beginning of the book sets him off on a quest. Even more relevant for Wagner was the use of the dream world by E.T.A. Hoffmann, the author whose views on music he found so revealing. In the introduction to one of his most bizarre tales, *Die Elixiere des Teufels* (*The Devil's Elixirs*), Hoffmann writes: 'what we call simply dream and imagination might represent the secret thread that runs through our lives'.[6] It was such a secret thread that Senta recognized when the Dutchman appeared before her.

The culmination of the opera is the Dutchman's death, which is seen as a release and a fulfilment. Once again this was a central notion for German Romantic writers, particularly for Novalis, whose cycle of poems *Hymns to the Night* constitutes a celebration of death. Only beyond mortal existence is it possible for the spirit to be fully absorbed in the totality of the universe. The state that is only intimated in dreaming can be fully achieved in death.

Even in the original legend the Dutchman's goal was death. It was perhaps for this reason that his ship was sometimes envisaged as a death ship, as did Coleridge in *The Rime of the Ancient Mariner*. For Wagner, this part of the legend does not appear to have been of central interest, although in his stage directions he emphasizes the eerie circumstances of the appearance of his spectral ship and crew. In Berlin, where Wagner submitted his opera, the standards of scene painting had been revolutionized by Karl Friedrich Schinkel, the great Prussian architect who had designed a stupendous set for Mozart's *Die Zauberflöte* in 1816. Schinkel had encouraged many accomplished painters to enter this field, including the brilliant landscapist Karl Blechen, who designed sets for works by Hoffmann and Weber. In Dresden, where *Der fliegende Holländer* was first performed, artists of high standard were also employed by the theatre; they included the celebrated painter of folk scenes and idyllic landscapes, Adrian Ludwig Richter. Such artists were well versed in the associative use of natural forms. Richter, Blechen and Schinkel, indeed, had all been

---

6   E.T.A. Hoffmann, *The Devil's Elixirs*, trans. R. Taylor (London: Oneworld Classics, 2008), p. 4.

deeply impressed by the symbolic landscapes of the greatest German painter of the age, Caspar David Friedrich. Friedrich himself never undertook scene painting, but his use of imagery suggests interests akin to those found in Wagner's directions. Loneliness and the longing for death can frequently be found in his work. He often used the image of a ship coming into harbour to suggest the approach of death: a remarkable instance is *Die Lebensstufen* (The Stages of Life), in which an old man is beckoned towards the shore where a ghostly ship awaits him, silhouetted against the evening sky. Friedrich probably knew about the traditional image of the ship of death since he came from a sea port in Pomerania, where the legend was well known.

The death of Wagner's Dutchman, however, is far removed from the visions of Friedrich. It is a *Liebestod*, a culmination of love in death. Audiences of today perhaps identify less with Senta's determined self-sacrifice than with the Dutchman's sense of alienation. Isolation is no longer the prerogative of the artist. For all his fascination with the eerie sounds of the storm and the sea, Wagner drew his deepest inspiration from the psychological roots of the myth. It is his insight into the human qualities of his characters in the story, as much as its fantastic element, that makes for such excellent theatre.

How Wagner Found the Flying Dutchman

Mike Ashman

In December 1842 a local arts journal reported the preparation of a new work at the Saxon Court Opera in Dresden. 'A second opera by Richard Wagner, who has become famous overnight through his *Rienzi*, is being energetically rehearsed for production [...] it is entitled *Der fliegende Holländer,* and Wagner has combined Heine's fantastic story and the English narrative with some additions of his own.'[1]

The 'fantastic story' was by the German poet Heinrich Heine, who had an affectionate obsession for all things Dutch. Heine's *From the Memoirs of Herr von Schnabelewopski* (1834) has his travelling hero discover the Dutchman legend as a play in an Amsterdam theatre: 'You will all be familiar with the story of that doom-laden ship, which can never enter the shelter of a port and which has now been roaming the seas since time immemorial. That dreadful ship bore its captain's name, a Dutchman who once swore by all the devils that he would round some cape or other in spite of the most violent storm which was raging – even if he had to keep sailing until the Day of Judgement.'[2]

If the legend of the Flying Dutchman has any basis in fact, it surely grew out of events in the Anglo-Dutch trade rivalry and wars of the seventeenth and eighteenth centuries, the period when Dutch merchantmen were regularly rounding South Africa's Cape of Good Hope. (A 2002 Dutch television documentary even wondered whether the phrase 'Vliegende Hollander' was a corruption of the

---

1   *Zeitung für die elegante Welt.*
2   Heinrich Heine, 'Aus den Memoiren des Herrn Schnabelewopski', *Sämtliche Werke*, vol. 3 (Philadelphia: Verlag von John Weik & Co., 1860), p. 91.

name 'Vergulde Vlamingh' ['Gold-plated Fleming'], a hard-driving Dutch sea captain of that era.) Later, from the 1790s, coincidentally a flood of poems and stories in English and American literature started to appear treating the theme of a cursed sailor on an eternal voyage. Samuel Taylor Coleridge's *The Rime of the Ancient Mariner*, Sir Walter Scott's *Rokeby,* James Fenimore Cooper's *The Red Rover* and Edgar Allan Poe's *The Narrative of Arthur Gordon Pym of Nantucket* are perhaps the best crafted of what that Dresden correspondent rightly called 'the English narrative' version of the legend.

At first the play which Heine's hero attends looks like a straight retelling of the legend, but then it suggests a way out for the doomed Dutchman: 'The Devil took the ship's captain at his word and he is forced to roam the seas until Judgement Day unless he be saved by a woman's devotion. In his stupidity the Devil does not believe in woman's devotion and so allowed the doomed captain to go ashore once every seven years, to marry and in that way to seek his salvation.'[3] So Heine's Schnabelewopski gets to see 'Mrs Flying Dutchman' fling herself off a cliff-top, as a result of which 'the curse is lifted, the Dutchman is saved, and we see the ghostly ship sinking into the depths of the ocean'.[4]

Heine intended this new twist to the ending as a mickey-take of what he regarded as a sentimental and romanticized ghost story. 'The moral of this piece, as far as women are concerned,' he concludes, 'is that they should be careful of marrying a Flying Dutchman; and we men can see from the piece how, in the best of circumstances, women are the ruin of us all.'[5] But Wagner took the possibility of the Dutchman's salvation very seriously indeed, noting in 'An Autobiographic Sketch': 'it was especially [Heine's] treatment of the redemption of this Ahasuerus of the seas – borrowed from a Dutch play under the same title – that placed within my hands all the material for turning the legend into an opera subject. I obtained the consent of Heine himself [...]'[6]

---

3   Ibid., p. 91.
4   Ibid., p. 94.
5   Ibid., p. 94.
6   'Autobiographic Sketch', *Richard Wagner's Prose Works*, trans. William Ashton Ellis, 8 vols. (London: Kegan Paul, Trench, Trübner & Co., 1892–99), vol 1., p. 17 (trans. modified).

It was in Paris that Wagner had met Heine, another exiled German intellectual who briefly befriended him during several years of penniless living and (despite a letter of commendation from the powerful and well-established Meyerbeer) failure to make his name in the French capital. After the conversation between poet and composer, Heine predicted about Wagner that 'from an individuality so replete with modern culture, it is possible to expect the development of a solid and powerful modern music'.[7] The first notes of a 'solid and powerful modern music' were certainly heard in the *Holländer* score, where Wagner explored the art of characterization by harmonic language as well as by colour, rhythm and tempo: a dramatic, modern chromaticism for the Dutchman himself, his suffering and his would-be rescuer Senta, and a rum-ti-tum old-style, grand operatic diatonicism for the bourgeois domesticity of Daland, Mary and the spinning girls. When Wagner began the music of the new opera in Paris, he was hoping for a successful audition with some of its numbers at the famed Opéra. He was to end up with nothing but a small amount of money from selling his scenario for the work to their management.

Heine's story, his meeting with the author and the life of a struggling artist in Paris were important spurs to Wagner's *Holländer* project, but there was also an autobiographical, 'on-site' element to the story. If Wagner first read Heine's story during his music directorship in Riga, it would have been fresh in his mind during the interrupted sea voyage he made from Russia to France in the summer of 1839. This journey cast Wagner, almost literally, upon the shore of the southern Norwegian coast at the very spot (Sandvika on the island of Borøya) where his opera would eventually be set. Although Norwegian researchers have tried hard to match the skimpy details of Wagner's two-day stay with the *Holländer* libretto, it can at present only be said with safety that the *Thetis* (his ship) did indeed shelter at Borøya from a ferocious storm that July, and that the island's granite cliffs make up an echoing wall that may have inspired the echo calls of the sailors' chorus in the opera's opening scene.

---

7   Heinrich Heine quoted in: Ferdinand Praeger, *Wagner As I Knew Him*, (London and New York: Longmans, Green and Co., 1892), p. 92.

However, the importance of Norway to the opera went beyond literal influences. Until only weeks before the *Holländer*'s January 1843 premiere, the action had been set in Scotland (Act One took place at 'Holystrand', Senta was Anna, her father Donald or just 'the Scotsman', and Erik was Georg). This was presumably because not only the Heine story but also a best-selling German horror story of the time, which Wagner knew, called *Die Höhle von Steenfoll* (The Cave of Steenfoll) and a popular contemporary musical (probably known to Heine) called *The Flying Dutchman, or The Phantom Ship* were all set in Scotland, the remote mythical home of caves, wrecks and sea ghosts. Then (apparently) Wagner suddenly changed his mind and moved the story to Norway. Why? It may have been that he heard that an opera, inspired (not very closely) by the Dutchman sketch which he had sold, had just opened in Paris, and he wanted to distance his original from that project. Or he may have wanted to blur the issue of his debt to Heine. (Thirty years later Wagner's latest memoirs, *Mein Leben*, would omit mention altogether of the poet's 'own invention' of the redemption ending.) Or perhaps because it chimed with an idea he was beginning to develop: that the creation of a work should always be linked to 'real' events in a true artist's life. Later Wagner insisted that this 1843 'Romantic opera' was the true starting point of his career as poet and music dramatist, a belief embraced by the Bayreuth Festival which has always declined (until the bicentenary year 2013) to stage any of his earlier works.

Although the *Dutchman* made a dimmer impression at its Dresden premiere than had the bright star of the lengthy, loud and apparently more conventional *Rienzi*, the new work's eventual acceptance was guaranteed by the fact that Wagner had at last got his hands upon a genuinely popular subject. Aside from the work of the authors mentioned above, there were, in the first decades of the nineteenth century, two widely circulated (and translated) British novels – John Howison's *Vanderdecken's Message Home* (the first known text to name the ghostly captain) and Frederick Marryat's *The Phantom Ship* (which has a redemption ending and launched a mini-Flying Dutchman craze in Holland) – and a number of original or translated

Dutch plays (which Heine could actually have seen on his regular visits to the country). It is also no accident that the first vampire tales of Polidori and Byron, and Mary Shelley's *Frankenstein* are the exact contemporaries of these maritime ghost narratives of the Dutchman. Both these strands of story use the idea of the dead coming back to life, or characters being unable to die until some crime or sin committed in the past has been formally expiated. As Edward Fitzball, author of the *Phantom Ship* musical, noted in his memoirs: 'These sorts of drama were then very much in vogue, and *The Flying Dutchman* was not by any means behind even *Frankenstein* or *Der Freischütz* itself in horrors and blue fire.'[8]

Wagner's own libretto drew on features common to many versions of the phantom-ship story: the ghost crew's attempt to have letters delivered home to addressees who prove to be long dead (mocked by the Norwegian sailors in the quayside scene), the magical sailing properties of the Dutchman's bewitched ship (remarked upon by the Dutchman himself in the Sandvika scene), and the old family portrait of the Dutchman himself (ever present throughout the action inside Daland's house). In a breakthrough in his creation of a new operatic form parallel to his use of different harmonic language to stress characterization, Wagner was able to mix and match the influences and references from his reading with a novelist's insight. The recent scientific experiments of Mesmer with magnetism, and the Romantic fascination of the age with dreams and trances, find their place in his libretto in Senta's obsession with the Dutchman's portrait and her instant identification with the dream in which Erik predicts the action of the rest of the opera. Going beyond the simple idea of a life for a life proposed by the climax of Heine's story, Wagner arrived at a psychoanalytical perception of the central core of the Dutchman legend. His story becomes one of restoration in which the dreamer (the cursed sailor) has to be returned to his original, 'right' state of mind before his mad act of hubris (the oath to round the Cape at any cost). This restoration can only be achieved when a human being from 'normal' life

---

8   Edward Fitzball, *Thirty-Five Years of a Dramatic Author's Life*, 2 vols. (London: T. C. Newby, 1859), vol. 1, pp. 168–69.

comes to understand fully and to feel compassion for the action and sufferings of the dreamer.

Wagner also introduced influences from less specific sources. Ahasuerus's frustrated attempts at suicide in Nikolaus Lenau's epic poems about the Wandering Jew suggested the failure of the Dutchman (as told in his opening monologue) to run his ship aground or have himself killed by pirates. The placing and content of Senta's Ballad – some of the first music for the opera, composed in Paris – owe much to the heroine's ballad in Boieldieu's *La Dame blanche*, Act Two of which even begins with a spinning scene. Marschner, a contemporary whose scores Wagner both knew and conducted, set his *Der Vampyr* in Scotland. It includes a ballad sung by a local girl about the vampire legend which describes the anti-hero with the identical phrase Senta finds for the Dutchman, 'den bleichen Mann' ('the pale man', a common tag for the sexually desired undead in nineteenth-century literature). Putting his own wide reading and listening to fullest advantage, Wagner was not only able to make his *Der fliegende Holländer* a classic of what became known as the *Schauerromantik* genre, but to transcend his rivals, much as Shakespeare's *Hamlet* had done for Jacobean tragedy and Puccini's *Tosca* would for *verismo* opera.

Of Storms and Dreams

Reflections on the Stage History
of *Der fliegende Holländer*

Katherine Syer

Senta and the Dutchman are atypical operatic lovers. Mutual need and her acute sense of compassion supplant effusive emotion, so much so that their introspective, idealistic duet in Act Two hardly registers as the opera's gravitational centre. Erik misunderstands the situation as a demonically driven love triangle. His superstitious perspective nonetheless helps keep the Dutchman's supernatural aura in play. In shaping the legend of the cursed seafarer into a libretto, Wagner recognized that the fantastic dimensions of his existence would yield the opera's main fount of musical energy, as well as its most thrilling theatrical moments. The Dutchman, for his part, mostly endeavours to conceal his curse from the Norwegian community. Wagner, however, paced the drama so as repeatedly to spotlight the strange forces that envelop the Dutchman and his ship. The first such instance, the arrival of the ghostly vessel, encapsulates the drama's central idea of a static image or fictional portrait brought uncannily to life. With the main stage action grinding to a halt, and all the Norwegian characters asleep beneath calm skies, a localized gale blows the Dutchman's ship ashore at a terrifying pace. The contrasting realities are depicted with care in the score. Yet, when the opera's premiere was hastily produced in Dresden, in February 1843, the animation of large pieces of three-dimensional scenery could not be rendered persuasively by the normally proficient technical crew.

Wagner's own *Rienzi*, which had already proved popular the previous year and had been prepared more carefully, replaced *Der fliegende Holländer* after only four performances. As revival opportunities for his early nautical drama arose, Wagner was especially keen to solve the staging challenges of the Dutchman's ghostly ship.

Conspicuously absent from Wagner's primary dramatic source for his libretto is the scenario of the Dutchman's seemingly opportunistic arrival, with Daland's crew becalmed and the Steersman asleep. Already in his first completed opera, *Die Feen* (completed in 1834 and based on Carlo Gozzi's 1762 play *La donna serpente*),Wagner had developed a scene in which a supernatural figure magically materializes while another character sleeps onstage. His linking of manifestations of the supernatural with altered states of consciousness in *Holländer* – respectively sleep, dreams/somnambulism and drunkenness in the opera's three acts – is hardly original, but it is systematically pursued and flirts effectively with the notion of ambiguity. The eighteenth-century dramatic origins of *Die Feen* remind us that set changes during such sleep scenes could be achieved swiftly during that period by the switching of painted scenic drops. Wagner was also interested in attenuated processes involving illusions of perspective.

An early solution for the arrival of the Dutchman's ship, or later, of Lohengrin's swan, involved reduced-size versions of the magical vehicle appearing first in front of the backdrop. The full-sized boat or swan could then give the impression of having crossed a great distance quickly when it came into view downstage. The requirement of multiple visually realistic and yet movable ships in *Holländer*, one of which needed to bear live singing sailors, raised other concerns of scale that were not easily solved. Not even Heinrich Döll was able to achieve a fully satisfactory outcome in his designs for the outer acts of the 'model' production of December 1864 in Munich, which followed King Ludwig II's accession to the throne of Bavaria earlier that year. For decades thereafter, the opening scene of *Der fliegende Holländer* was typically a crowded, portrait-like image, with the sides of the proscenium framed by steep cliffs and a rocky foreground that partially camouflaged the resting of the ships in the water. The hard-to-achieve illusion of a sea in motion was managed through painted drop-cloths that could be animated by hand; the view of the water was in general somewhat restricted. Angelo Quaglio's designs for the interior setting in the 1864 Munich production exuded a contrasting simplicity. A handful of nautical images in addition to the portrait of the Dutchman kept the image of the sea alive in Daland's modest home. The opera's closing scene, with the Dutchman and Senta ascending transfigured, was another non-naturalistic stage effect for which reliance on 'realistic' imagery – effigies of the two characters rising in an embrace – often undercut the intended effect.

The storms and despair that plague the Dutchman recall a pair of works that entered Wagner's awareness with fresh urgency in 1840: Gluck's *Iphigénie en Aulide* (1774) and *Iphigénie en Tauride* (1779). Wagner reconsidered both operas as he wrote his essay devoted to opera overtures which was published early in 1841, shortly before he fleshed out his *Holländer* libretto from working prose drafts. Agamemnon's situation in the first of Gluck's *Iphigénie* operas overlaps with the Dutchman's through their pivotal acts of hubris: the Mycenaean king boasted of beating the goddess of hunting Diana at her own art and shot a deer in her sacred grove; the sea captain vowed he could overcome a terrible storm, ostensibly the embodiment of Satan's angry energies. Both men subsequently find themselves in impossible situations and rail at the mercilessness of higher powers. In *Iphigénie en Aulide*, the goddess first punishes Agamemnon by withholding the winds needed for his war fleet to set sail for Troy. The goddess eventually grants the return of gentle breezes in B flat major, the key of the favourable south winds that set Daland's ship back on course for home at the end of Act One of *Der fliegende Holländer*. The opening storm of Gluck's sequel, *Iphigénie en Tauride*, swells in B minor, a tonal area closely associated with the Dutchman. Gluck's tempestuous musical introduction is remarkable for its metaphoric potency and multiple meanings that resonate with Wagner's *Holländer*. Gluck's *Iphigénie* operas cannot be considered powerful models of overly ambitious staging practices, but they clearly offered Wagner potent ideas for coordinating the exterior and interior levels of his drama with music that bears a great deal of the dramatic meaning. They also encouraged him to explore the psychological experiences of his characters as powerful shaping agents.

In anticipation of Liszt's 1853 performances of *Der fliegende Holländer* in Weimar, Wagner wrote an essay which could be distributed to theatres that might perform the work.[1] For the most part he focused on the characterization of his principal quartet of dramatic figures. He dealt with scenographic matters summarily, steering designers and machinists to the directions published in the score. Still, he made sure to draw attention to the demands of the first act: the need to register the extraordinary and extreme nature of the storm and to chart detailed weather changes with lighting and painted scrims. Wagner's comments directed at singers reflect awareness that his recourse to generic character types, which he skewed in atypical directions, might actually encourage interpretations too squarely centred on the stereotypes. Take Senta's self-absorbed nature and somnambulistic tendencies, for example. Wagner inscribed the structure and content of some of her more outrageous expressions with recognizable behavioural symptoms of someone under the influence of hypnosis (or 'mesmerism', as it was known in Wagner's time). Then, as now, such behaviour can easily elicit sceptical responses, including the suspicion of charlatanism or a form of illness or weakness. Wagner's emphasis in his essay on Senta's solid and naive, if unusual, nature is awkward to digest, above all since she appears fully in command of her senses when she forfeits her life for the Dutchman. Senta's curiously strong constitution is perhaps best understood through the lens of Wagner's admiration for Iphigenia, as rendered in Gluck's operas and in Goethe's adaptation of Euripides' play, *Iphigenie auf Tauris*. Iphigenia does not resist her father's agreement that she be sacrificed in order to absolve him and lend support for an embattled Greek nation. Her willing self-abnegation resonates problematically in modern times, as does Senta's commitment to redeem the Dutchman – a driving factor in many contemporary revisionist stagings of Wagner's opera. The object of Senta's devotion often comes under sharp scrutiny as a result, with the Dutchman's similarity to actively predatory figures often surfacing in staged interpretations. For his part, Wagner

---

1   See pp. 65–72 [Ed.].

stressed in his written commentary the Dutchman's weariness and reluctance to participate once more in a seemingly futile game. And at the end, motivated by a misunderstanding, he releases Senta from her promise in an effort to protect her life. Wagner's detailed comments in the essay on the interpretation of the Dutchman's first scene give the impression that each musical gesture was conceived with a coordinating stage action in mind. Wagner's directions are above all a counter-directive to the way a dark, quasi-heroic protagonist might typically carry out his first stage entrance and aria, with more energy and perhaps blustery bravado than Wagner wanted his exhausted Dutchman initially to demonstrate.

Not until the later 1880s did a change in theatre technology begin to open up new possibilities for staging *Der fliegende Holländer*. Wagner himself experimented with the use of electric lighting for special effects before it became the principal means of stage illumination shortly after his death. Its bright, harsh quality, in comparison with the soft yellowish hue of gas lighting, could differentiate supernatural effects such as *Parsifal*'s glowing Grail from the surrounding illusionistic stage image. High-powered electric light sources also enabled the projection of images painted on glass slides, so long as they were not too detailed. Atmosphere and weather-related projections, along the lines of those that could be useful for *Holländer*, worked well in the inaugural 1876 *Ring* at Bayreuth. With the widespread use of electric lighting all aspects of theatre design were exposed to greater scrutiny in terms of nuance and detail. Fostering a design trend towards ever more realistic imagery, new strides in lighting technology also gradually supported experimentation with stylization and visual symbolism. Wagner's own theatre at Bayreuth was slow to pursue the latter directions. When *Holländer* was first performed in Wagner's Festspielhaus in 1901, it was essentially a more historically detailed variant of the production mounted in Munich in 1864, now in the one-act version favoured by Cosima, as originally intended but never realized by Wagner. Already an accomplished Wotan, the Dutch singer Anton van Rooy took on the role of the Dutchman, partnered by Emmy Destinn as Senta, and went on to become one of the great Wagnerian bass-baritones of his time. Cosima Wagner relied, as usual, on the designer Max Brückner for the basic set design. Special steam machinery that had been installed for the premiere of the *Ring* proved useful for supplying an eerie mist around the Dutchman's ship, which the composer's son Siegfried Wagner also enhanced with electric light when he directed the opera. The introduction of a rear curved backcloth, or cyclorama, for the short-lived 1914 revival opened up the stage picture of the outer acts onto a vast horizon.

The next new production of *Der fliegende Holländer* at Bayreuth did not occur until 1939 and this then lasted until 1942. It was the designer Emil Preetorius's last collaboration with the conductor and director Heinz Tietjen during the era of Winifred Wagner, Siegfried Wagner's widow. A designer of great sensitivity but cautious with regard to change, Preetorius at least brought Bayreuth into the orbit of contemporary production styles with his streamlined landscapes. His wooden cabin setting for Act Two completely rejected the formal, excessively detailed space that Cosima had presented. The lack of visual distraction set Maria Müller's notably penetrating interpretation of Senta in sharp relief. For these wartime performances Rudolf Bockelmann shared the role of the Dutchman with Jaro Prohaska and Joel Berglund.

Influential fresh approaches to the depiction of the Dutchman's ship had already emerged in the early decades of the twentieth century outside Bayreuth. In 1917, the designer Max Hasait in Dresden hit upon the solution of realizing the spectral vessel as a shadow. Using an intense light source and a miniature model of a ship not only proved cost-effective, but also easily created a silhouette that could appear swiftly and achieve imposing dimensions. Other designers seized on elements that could be treated as visually dominant or even pervasive, such as the ghostly ship's blood-red sail, or the sea. A red lightning-spiked backdrop was used for the opening scene in 1926 in Königsberg, for example. With Daland's ship nowhere to be seen and only black cliffs serving as contrast, the emergence of the Flying Dutchman from the watery depths yielded an overwhelmingly ominous impression. A few years earlier, in 1922, the director Oskar Fritz Schuh kept the imagery of the sea alive throughout the opera's second act by virtue of its being visible in the background. Many subsequent productions have manipulated Wagner's clear visual distinction between exterior and interior settings in significant ways.

By the later 1920s, fresh acting styles had also come to play a significant role in the changing image of *Holländer*. Jürgen Fehling, a director most familiar in the spoken theatre world in Berlin, brought an expressionistic touch to his 1929 Krolloper staging. Otto Klemperer opted to conduct the early Dresden version of the score, with its less glorified treatment of Senta's redemption of the Dutchman. Ewald Dülberg's cool, stylized design aesthetic erased all hints of Romantic naturalism in the outdoor settings. If such austere stage pictures reflected the spirit of the Bauhaus, the second act nodded more in the direction of Surrealism. Mist surrounded Senta's house as if it were suspended, with the black mast of the Dutchman's ship looming above. Senta was dressed in a modern grey skirt and blue pullover, with a shocking red wig that surely triggered associations with the expansive red sail of the ghost ship, above all when she sang her Ballad as if demonically possessed. Psychological strangeness was perfectly at home in a production with so few references to nature and cosy Norwegian life. Instead of spinning their wheels – a Romantic symbol *par excellence* – the female chorus mended fishing nets by hand. Many a director has since bypassed *Holländer*'s spinning wheels. The Krolloper production's subsequent iconic status is very much linked to the politically motivated and divisive responses it provoked, and to the institution's demise at the hands of the Nazis, but its artistically progressive thrust has proved long-lived.

Difficult times as they were, the years following the Second World War were also intensively creative ones for many theatres, especially in East Germany. Tight budgets could encourage directors and designers to do more with less. Lighting and projection technology offered increasingly sophisticated options. In these years, opera's reputation as an elite genre – one sometimes focused on singing at the expense of overall theatrical value – prompted a wave of directors and designers to bring more exacting dramatic standards to their work. Walter Felsenstein became renowned and reviled for the liberties he took with published stage directions in the name of a dramaturgically rigorous and realistic kind of music theatre. His years at the helm of East Berlin's Komische Oper (1947–75) supported the development of some of the next generation's most active Wagner directors: Joachim Herz, Götz Friedrich and Harry Kupfer. The Bayreuth Festival had meanwhile reopened in 1951, earlier than many felt was appropriate given its intimate ties with Hitler and the Nazi Party. Wieland Wagner was determined to reclaim his grandfather's stage, with a production style that was completely different from what had been seen in Bayreuth in the 1930s and early 1940s. He justified his Spartan visual aesthetic by his grandfather's interest in Greek theatre, while grounding design-related decisions and matters of characterization in Jung-influenced psychological exegeses. His brother Wolfgang Wagner's more tempered hand steered *Holländer* back onto the Bayreuth stage in 1955 with simplified but referential designs. Wieland's first staging of the work, in 1959, erupted as a theatrically charged *non sequitur*, and a telling indication that he was not wholly devoted to a politically correct remythologization of Wagner's oeuvre.

We will probably never clearly understand the complexities of Wieland's evolution as an opera director and designer, nor the ways in which he absorbed the realities of his privileged existence during the Nazi years. The two were related. His recourse to the spirit of Greek drama initially helped him achieve some much-needed historical distance, but it must be remembered that Hellenism itself played a significant role in German nationalism, Wagner's included. *Holländer* was the last of Wagner's operas to be produced by Wieland, and the first for which he combined realistic imagery and lively stage action, in ways that fully responded to the dynamism of the score. The deck of Daland's ship filled the stage in Act One, with the crew rallying around the helm during the storm. Shrewdly, Wieland used the audience as the chorus's virtual focal point. That way, the Dutchman's ancient boat could appear from behind while the sailors onstage remained unaware of its presence. The audience saw the projection of the time-worn planks of a large hull, which could be likened to human ribs, upon which the wild mariner was pinioned. Wieland had explored related imagery in the curved columns that framed the tortured Amfortas during *Parsifal*'s Grail scenes. Wieland's decision to use the original Dresden score of *Holländer* was tied to his critique of redemption as inscribed in the end of the work. His Dutchman died on stage, while Senta disappeared from view. The Dutchman's crew of undead sailors, by extension, remained unredeemed, having been rendered visible in their showdown with the Norwegian sailors. Wieland approached Daland, the character most impervious to the mythic level of the drama, as a sharply contrasting comic caricature, rejecting Wagner's 1852 caution against just such a portrayal. Walter Panofsky interpreted the result as a Pantalone figure, which is intriguing given that one of the dramaturgical models for Act One of *Der fliegende Holländer* was the opening act of Carlo Gozzi's play *Il corvo* (*The Raven*), which the composer's uncle Adolph Wagner had translated as *Der Rabe* (1804). The captain of that tale's ship, which is temporarily harboured by a storm, is none other than Pantalone – a somewhat unlikely role for the Venetian *commedia* figure more typically known for his pecuniary concerns and interest in a profitable marriage arrangement for his daughter. Especially in his later production of *Meistersinger* (1963), Wieland pursued comic strains in Wagner's works in order to expose the uncritical worshipful attitudes of Bayreuth audiences. His decision to end the Dutchman's intense suffering in death on stage may reflect back critically on his own life experiences. Anja Silja, who sang Senta in the 1960 revival of Wieland's production and became his mistress and muse during the remaining six years of his life, has openly acknowledged the unresolved inner demons that haunted him.

Wagner reached the stage of Felsenstein's Komische Oper in Berlin for the first time in 1962. Joachim Herz's production of *Holländer* there had an unusual legacy, beginning with a revival in Moscow the following year (no Wagner opera had been staged there for over twenty years). In this interpretation, updated to Wagner's time, Daland's bourgeois affluence was portrayed as stifling, thereby justifying Senta's inclination towards escapist fantasies. Adapting his stage concept for a film made in Leipzig in 1964, Herz capitalized on the wide format of CinemaScope to depict Senta's outdoor, light-infused dream world. (By contrast, in his 1975 version filmed for BBC television, the director Brian Large shrouded the Dutchman's world in a cool blue light, while the Norwegians were shown in full colour.) Herz effected the transitions to and from the contrasting normal, narrower-screen realistic world with various montage techniques, after launching the entire narrative as a self-conscious slide into a fictional world of story-telling. The framing strategy of Senta as a book-reading escapist has been repeated many times since, although rarely leading to the conclusion found in Herz's film: Senta flees her oppressive surroundings and is seen running towards the sun as it rises in the background.

Harry Kupfer's 1978 Bayreuth production of *Der fliegende Holländer* became one of the most widely known interpretations of the opera after it was made commercially available on VHS in 1985, and subsequently on DVD. Working with his designer Peter Sykora, Kufper also pursued an interpretation that distinguished Senta's perspective while exploiting a range of polarities that are built into the work. They developed a dynamic unit set whose main arrangement was an unfriendly, tall, brick-walled room, with a lone window to the outside world placed up high, far beyond the reach of the dour ladies below. A staircase on the side of the room led up to the window, which Lisbeth Balslev as Senta in the first years of the production negotiated while desperately clutching the Dutchman's portrait. From this vantage point, with Senta remaining on stage as the hallucinatory wellspring, the walls of the room rapidly moved to accommodate the action of the exterior scenes involving the Dutchman and his ship.

Kupfer's entrance scene for Simon Estes's Dutchman developed Wieland Wagner's treatment of the ancient vessel into a movable set piece with stronger religious overtones. The ribbed ship's hull was articulated as praying hands which opened to reveal Estes standing on deck with his arms spread wide, chained crucifix-like to one of the ship's beams. The sense of physical exhaustion as he crumbled to the ground was overwhelming. The dark, undefined figure that Daland brought to his home in Act Two proved to be a projection of Senta's personal obsession. In contrast to Herz's approach, but sharing its socially critical angle, Senta's psychological world had no obviously pleasurable dimension in Kupfer's staging, especially when she leapt through the window to her death at the end. In a similar vein, Keith Warner's 1998 Brighton production, sung in English, for New Sussex Opera also centred on an interpretation of Senta's behaviour as that of an incurable hysteric.

In 1975, in San Francisco, Jean-Pierre Ponnelle had used the sleepy character of the Steersman in Act One as the point of entry into an individual dream/nightmare-story interpretation (the production was revived at the Metropolitan Opera, New York, in 1979). Assuming the role of Erik within his nocturnal drama, the Steersman was relieved to awaken at the end after glimpsing Senta's utterly strange behaviour in his dream. Some later directors have placed Erik in an active role at the drama's conclusion, with him killing Senta in a fit of frustration and vengeance or enacting a self-determined mercy killing based on his perception of the Dutchman as Satan incarnate.

The idea of the fantastic elements of the narrative playing out in a mainly psychological space was also at work in the 1981 Munich production directed and designed by Herbert Wernicke. The action began in a large white room, whose draped furniture initially provided little in the way of historical orientation. The comforting environment, reflective of Biedermeier domesticity, was gradually revealed as what Wernicke's Dutchman yearned for, and precisely what Senta hoped, in vain, to escape through him. This attempt to treat the set as a mental *tabula rasa* for the Dutchman and his quest was not well received by Munich audiences at the time, accustomed as they might have been to the overtly old-fashioned film adaptation directed by Václav Kašlík in 1974 in that city's film studios. The spirit of Wernicke's *Holländer* could be felt in Willy Decker's production for Oper Köln in 1991, subsequently seen in Paris in 2000. Decker's designer, Wolfgang Gussmann, was sensitive to the inherent dangers of setting a stormy drama in such a cool, sterile environment. The action of the opera was placed in the corner of a large white room, at the intersection of two visible walls. One was graced by a large door; the other had a recessed area in which the Dutchman's portrait hung. The broad canvas periodically sprang to life, revealing new points of emphasis or even images. In Act Three, the Dutchman's crew magically appeared on the canvas, bathed in red light, while the Norwegian sailors looked on, frozen in cool blue – the colour of light that often entered the room by way of the large door serving as a portal to the supernatural world. The Dutchman's departure through that door marked the collapse of Senta's dream. She then took her own life with a knife while standing one last time before the painting. A young girl meanwhile came into the picture in such a way as to suggest that she was to be the next Senta.

Dieter Dorn's 1990 Bayreuth production pulled back from Kupfer's dark and intensely psychological portrait through Jürgen Rose's stylized designs, but also proved to be highly attuned to theatricality and precision stagecraft. Artificiality was expressed through colour as well as form. Daland's house, for example, was a small-scale white shell, with an interior saturated in caustic yellow that matched the full moon in the sky above. During their duet, the Dutchman and Senta stepped out of the domestic shape into the black surrounding space. Suspended above the stage floor, the house began to rotate as a visual metaphor for Senta's world being turned upside down. The light bulb, hanging naked, and chair upon which the Dutchman placed his hat were special markers that remained perfectly in place as the form turned a full 360 degrees. Richard Jones, in his 1993 production with the designer Nigel Lowery in Amsterdam, achieved even more peculiarly self-conscious visual effects. The next production of *Holländer* at Bayreuth, directed by Claus Guth in 2006, continued the focus on theatricality and featured John Tomlinson singing his first Dutchman. Critics noted the prefatory pantomime of Daland reading a storybook to his young daughter and seized upon the visual doubling of the Norwegian sea captain and the Dutchman as a cue that child abuse was implied. Guth's recourse to doubles, including puppet-like forms, in fact permeated the production as well as Christian Schmidt's set – an Ibsenesque interior with some of its elements mirrored on either side of a sweeping staircase. Shadowy projections evoked seascapes on the lower half of the stage while the upper half was marked as a theatrical space, above all by red drapery. With no credible lifelike figure or natural environment visible, the Dutchman's eventual retreat behind the door at the edge of the theatrical curtain cemented the crushing sense that Senta was utterly alone.

Given *Holländer*'s repeated references to the sea, a production mounted on the massive floating stage at the Bregenz Festival, on Lake Constance, seemed an obvious choice. The first production of *Holländer* there was directed by Luca Ronconi in 1973, and incorporated real ships. In 1989, the director David Pountney and designer Stefanos Lazaridis pursued a more indirect interpretative approach by forging a strong connection between the water and Senta's fluid psychological realm. The stage itself bore many industrial allusions to underscore Daland's materialistic orientation. Pountney had worked earlier with Lazaridis, his regular collaborator, on a production in English during the early 'Power House' years at English National Opera. Then, too, they explored unusual dramatic possibilities in the form of a stage revolve, while attention to Daland's wealth manifested itself in the atmosphere of a splendid mansion. In his most recent engagement with *Holländer*, at Welsh National Opera in 2006, Pountney bypassed the sea as a central metaphor and instead explored the idea of outer space as the endless realm in which the Dutchman has so often wandered. The production featured the role debut in London of Bryn Terfel as the Dutchman. Set designer Robert Innes Hopkins worked with video artists Jane and Louis Wilson on a core element of the set: two large flat projection surfaces angled slightly outward, prowlike, at their hinge. On these surfaces flashed allusions to spacecraft, as well as intimate close-ups of the Dutchman and Senta. This latest reading of Wagner's opera by Pountney was especially strong in its portrayal of women in the opera being abused or treated as subservient. The members of the female chorus were sexually overcome with force by their men in Act Three, while Senta's willingness to redeem the Dutchman was critically interpreted as a form of blind missionary zeal.

Violence began to erupt in productions of *Holländer* from the mid-1970s. In Ulrich Melchinger's 1976 Kassel staging, the Dutchman was shown to rape a woman with his sword, thereby killing her, during his monologue. Nothing in Wagner's opera explicitly lends itself to such an interpretation: the stereotype of a vampire-like protagonist looms large, but the drama resists the idea of a violent figure. Even Erik, whom the women taunt as hot-blooded, defies typecasting efforts. His concern that Senta is sexually vulnerable (consciously or otherwise) can also be seen as unfounded. Nevertheless, the appetite of some directors for degradation and violence has become increasingly unrestrained, as seen in Calixto Bieito's 2008 production of *Holländer* in Stuttgart and Michael von zur Mühlen's staging in Leipzig the same year.

Mike Ashman's updated production of *Der fliegende Holländer* at Covent Garden in 1986 explored contemporary visual equivalents for the opera's spectrum of characters without dwelling on negative implications. Neither did he obliterate the drama's carefully structured play of contrasts. Ashman's Daland was a dapper businessman, his Dutchman the operator of a dilapidated boat. Peter Konwitschny's placement of Wagner's spinning ladies atop cycling equipment in Moscow and Munich in 2004 and 2006 moved the action into a high-spirited present, under bright lights, but concluded with a markedly pessimistic scene in which Senta was depicted as a suicide bomber. Director Martin Kušej had Erik kill both Senta and the Dutchman at the end of their 2010 production in Amsterdam, following a string of scenes in which the simple shape of the drama and its basic elements were deliberately muddled.

Of the few recent directors to see some positive redemptive value in the opera's ending, Götz Friedrich deserves special mention here. At the Deutsche Oper in Berlin, in 1997, he staged *Der fliegende Holländer* for the first time, after directing all of Wagner's other mature operas on numerous occasions in various European opera houses. Gottfried Pilz's designs alluded sporadically to German life from the years just following the Second World War through to the present, as with the construction cranes so familiar to Berliners in the years following reunification. Senta's self-sacrifice, in this instance, was shown to redeem not a problematic individual but a crowd of grey-clad men and women at the end – an obviously recognizable population indeed for Friedrich's audience.

Wagner's 1852 attempt to steer directors and singers away from interpretations of Senta as a victim has found few adherents in recent decades. Her relationship to the Dutchman is one that almost no contemporary staging celebrates unequivocally. At the same time, approaches focusing on the stereotypes that undoubtedly lie beneath Wagner's subtly adjusted characters offer insight into the creative process of a progressive artist who sometimes over-estimated his achievements. The theatrical vitality of his *Holländer* continues to be appreciated in a variety of revisionist interpretations, with modern technology opening up new ways of bringing the opera's supernatural and psychological realms to life.

The Overture to
Der fliegende Holländer (1852)[1]

Richard Wagner
translated by Melanie Karpinski

During his early years of exile following the failure of the 1849
Dresden revolution, Wagner wrote several programme notes about
Der fliegende Holländer *and* Tannhäuser.

The dreaded ship of the 'Flying Dutchman' flies on the wings of
the storm [1, 2, 3]; it nears the coast and drops anchor, for it is
here that its captain has been promised salvation [4]; we hear the
piteous strains of this message of redemption, which sound like a
mixture of prayer and complaint [5]. The doomed man listens to
them sullenly, bereft of hope: tired and longing for death, he steps
onto dry land, while his exhausted crew, weary of life, brings the
ship silently to rest. How often has this unhappy man already been
through this scene! How often has he steered his ship towards land,
where once in seven years it is granted him to step ashore; how
often has he hoped to find the end to his torment, and oh! – how
often has he found his hopes dashed and returned to his frenzied
wanderings across the seas! In order to force his destruction he
deliberately fought against billow and storm, steering his ship
into the raging abyss – yet here it was not dashed to pieces. All
the terrible dangers of the sea which once he scorned in his lust
for victorious adventure now laugh at him – they cannot harm

---

1   Richard Wagner, *Gesammelte Schriften und Dichtungen*, 10 vols. (Leipzig:
Breitkopf und Härtel, 1871–83), vol. 5, pp. 176–77.

him, for he is cursed to sail the seas forever, hunting for spoils which cannot thrill him, and never to find that which alone could redeem him!

A stately ship sweeps past him; he hears the joyful song of the sailors who are happy to be nearing home [10, 11]: he is consumed with anger at such merriment and, borne by the storm, he flashes past furiously, frightening and silencing the happy singers and putting the crew to flight [2, 7]. He cries out for salvation from the depths of his misery: in the lifeless desert of his lone existence only a wife can bring him release [4, 6, 9]! But where does his rescuer live? Where does a heart beat in sympathy for him? Where is the one who will not flee from him in horror and fear, like these cowardly men, who make the sign of the cross at his arrival? A glimmer of light then breaks through his darkness and pierces his tormented soul like lightning [12]. It dies away, and then rekindles: the seaman keeps the lodestar firmly in sight and steers determinedly through storm and wave towards it. What draws him so powerfully is the look of a woman which is full of sublime sadness and heaven-sent sympathy, which forces its way through to him! A heart has opened its unending depths to the sufferings of the doomed man: it must sacrifice itself to him, it must break with compassion and destroy itself in order to put an end to his misery. The cursed man breaks down at the sight of this divine vision, as his ship is dashed to pieces and engulfed by the ocean. He then rises, transfigured, from the waves, led by her victorious, rescuing hand towards the dawning of sublimest love.

Remarks on Performing the Opera
Der fliegende Holländer (1852)[1]

Richard Wagner
translated by Melanie Karpinski

*Wagner wrote the following in December 1852 in response to
a request by Franz Liszt, who was preparing a performance of*
Der fliegende Holländer *in Weimar the following year.*

First of all, I must remind both the conductor and the producer of
what I stressed so strongly with regard to the production of *Tannhäuser*: namely, the closest unity between what happens in the orchestra and what happens on stage. The ships and the sea, especially,
demand an enormous amount of attention from the producer: he will
find all the necessary indications at the corresponding places of the
pianoforte edition or full score. The first scene has to evoke the mood
of the opera in such a way that it becomes possible for the audience to
grasp the concept of the mysterious figure of the 'Flying Dutchman'
themselves: therefore it must be handled with exceptional care and
sympathy; the sea between the headlands must be seen to rage and
foam as much as possible; the representation of the ship cannot be
too naturalistic: little touches, such as the heaving of the ship when
struck by an exceptionally strong wave (during the two verses of
the Steersman's song) must be very clearly portrayed. The constant
subtle changes in lighting demand special care; in order to render as
effective as possible the nuances in weather in the first act, the skilful
use of painted gauzes to reach as far as centre stage is indispensable.

1   Ibid., pp. 160–68.

65

However, since these remarks are not specially directed to the purely decorative aspect of the performance (for which I must refer to the scenery of the opera as produced at the Schauspielhaus in Berlin) I am content, as stated, to plead for exact observation of my scattered scenic indications, while leaving the way they are carried out to the inventive powers of the scene-painter and the stage technician.

I shall therefore simply concern myself with the performers, and among these, more particularly with the representative of the very difficult principal male role of the Dutchman. The real success of the whole opera depends on the skilful presentation of the title role: its exponent must succeed in arousing and sustaining the greatest pity, and he will be able to do so if he observes the following main characteristics in his performance. His outward appearance has been sufficiently described. His first entry is extremely ceremonious and solemn: his slowness and hesitance when stepping onto dry land form a stark contrast to the unnatural speed of his ship over the sea. During the deep trumpet notes (B minor), at the very end of the introductory scene, he has stepped off the deck, along a plank lowered by one of the crew, to a shelf of rock on the shore: the first notes of the *ritornello* in the aria (the deep E sharp of the basses) accompany the Dutchman's first step ashore; his rolling gait, which is peculiar to sailors who have spent a long time away at sea, is accompanied by a wavelike figure for the cellos and violas; with the first crotchet of the third bar he takes his second step, still with folded arms and bowed head; the third and fourth steps coincide with the first notes of the eighth and tenth bars.

From this point on, his movements will naturally follow his general delivery, yet the performer must, under no pretext, be led astray into striding violently around the stage but must rather maintain a certain awe-inspiring calm in his outward demeanour, even during his most passionate expression of inner anguish and despair – in this way he will achieve the most effective characterization. His first phrases should be sung without the slightest emotion, as by one completely exhausted (almost in strict beat, like the whole of this recitative); even at the words 'Ha, stolzer Ozean' ('Ha! Haughty Ocean'), which are sung with bitter fury, he does not betray any passion, but merely half turns his head in the direction of the sea with an expression of terrible scorn.

During the *ritornello*, after 'doch ewig meine Qual' ('but my doom is eternal'), he bows his head once more, as though in utter weariness and despair; he sings, 'Euch, des Weltmeers Fluten' ('To you, surging ocean'), in this position, staring blankly before him. I should not like to cramp the singer too much in what he does during the *allegro* ('Wie oft in Meeres tiefsten Schrund' ['How often into ocean's deepest maw']), but he must adhere to my main directives: namely, that however deep the passion, and however agonized the anguish with which he instils the vocal line, he must retain the greatest outward composure: a simple arm or hand movement – not too sweeping – will suffice to emphasise the more dramatic moments. Even the words 'Niemals der Tod, nirgends ein Grab' ('Death never comes, nowhere a grave'),[2] which must be sung with the most powerful emphasis, belong more to the description of his sufferings than to a direct and real outburst of his despair: he only reaches this with what follows, for which the most energetic action must therefore be reserved. With the repetition of the words 'Dies der Verdammnis Schreckgebot' ('This is the dread sentence of damnation'), he bows both his head and his body quite deeply, and he remains in this position during the first four bars of the postlude: with the tremolo of the violins (E flat) at the fifth bar he raises his eyes towards heaven, while his body remains bent low; with the entry of the muffled drum roll at the ninth bar of the postlude, he begins to shudder uncontrollably and clench his fists convulsively at his sides, his lips trembling as he finally begins the phrase, 'Dich frage ich' ('I ask thee'), still staring fixedly towards heaven. The whole of this, almost direct, address to the 'Engel Gottes' ('angel from heaven'), for all the awesome expression with which it is to be sung, must still be delivered in the position just indicated (without any marked change beyond what the execution necessarily demands at certain places): we must see before us a 'fallen angel' himself, whose fearful torment drives him to proclaim his wrath against Eternal Justice. Finally, with the words 'Vergeb'ne Hoffnung' ('Vain hope'), however, the full force of his despair finds

---

2   The phrases are reversed in the printed libretto [Ed.].

expression: he stands tall and straight in his fury, his eyes still staring towards Heaven, and with the utmost energy of grief he casts all 'vain hope' behind: he no longer wants to hear of promised release, and (with the entry of the timpani and basses) he crumples together on the floor, as if destroyed. With the opening of the *allegro-ritornello*, his features revive with a new and terrible last hope, the hope of the World's destruction, in which he too would die. This closing *allegro* requires the most terrible energy, not only in the vocal phrasing, but also in his gesture, for everything here is unmasked passion. Yet the singer must take pains to make this whole section, despite its vehemence of phrasing, seem but a mere gathering of all his forces for the final crushing outbreak at the words, 'Ihr Welten, endet euren Lauf' ('You stars above, cease your course'), where he must reach a sublime climax. After the closing words, 'Ew'ge Vernichtung, nimm mich auf' ('Eternal extinction, fall on me'), he remains standing up straight, almost like a statue, throughout the whole *fortissimo* of the postlude: only with the *piano*, during the muffled chorus from the ship's hold, does he gradually relax his attitude: his arms sink to his sides; exhausted, he lowers his head at the four bars of *espressivo* for the first violins, and during the last eight bars of the postlude he walks unsteadily to the cliff face at the side; he leans his back against it and remains long in this position, his arms folded across his chest.

I have dealt with this scene in such detail in order to show the way I would like to have the Dutchman portrayed, and what weight I place on the most careful matching of the action to the music. The performer should take great pains to portray the rest of his role similarly. Moreover, this aria is the most difficult of the whole role, because the audience's further understanding of the subject depends upon the success of this scene: if this monologue has touched and penetrated the sympathy of the hearer as it should do, then the further success of the whole work is, for the most part, ensured – whereas nothing that comes later could possibly make up for anything neglected here.

In the following scene with Daland, the Dutchman remains initially in his previous position. He only raises his head slightly while answering Daland's questions from aboard the ship. When Daland approaches him, on land, the Dutchman also advances to about the middle of the stage, with stately calm. His whole demeanour here expresses quiet, peaceful dignity; the expression of his voice is calm and noble, without a hint of stronger accent: he reacts and speaks here as from the force of old habit: he has already experienced so many similar encounters and conversations; everything, even the apparently purposeful questions and answers are made only half-consciously; he reacts as if under the constraint of his position, to which he submits mechanically and without interest, like one exhausted. Just as instinctively his old yearning for redemption rekindles, after his terrible outburst of despair he now appears milder and softer, and he expresses his longing for peace with touching sadness. He throws out the question, 'Hast du eine Tochter?' ('Have you a daughter?), still with apparent calm; Daland's enthusiastic answer, 'Fürwahr, ein treues Kind' ('Indeed, a loving child') suddenly reawakens the old hope in him (so often proved to be futile): he cries out in almost frenzied haste, 'Sie sei mein Weib' ('Let her be my wife). He is once more caught by the old longing and describes his fate in the most poignant manner (remaining outwardly calm) with the words, 'Ach, ohne Weib, ohne Kind bin ich' ('Ah, I have no wife or child'). The glowing colours in which Daland now paints his daughter revive more keenly the Dutchman's old yearning for 'salvation through a woman's fidelity', and in the duet's closing *allegro* the battle between hope and despair rises to the height of passion, in which hope seems almost to prevail.

In his first appearance before Senta in the second act, the Dutchman's outward demeanour once more expresses complete calm and dignity: all his passionate emotions have been firmly imprisoned within him. Throughout the lengthy first *fermata* he remains motionless beside the door; at the beginning of the timpani solo he slowly advances downstage; with the eighth bar of this solo he stops (the two bars' *accelerando* for the strings relate to the gestures of Daland, who still stands surprised at the door, awaiting Senta's welcome, and he impatiently invites it with a movement of his outstretched arms); during the next three bars for the timpani, the Dutchman advances as far downstage as possible, where he now remains motionless, his eyes fixed on Senta. (The recurrence of the figure for the strings relates to the emphatic repetition of Daland's gesture: at the *pizzicato* on the next *fermata* he ceases to beckon to her, and shakes his head in amazement; with the entry of the basses after the *fermata*, he himself approaches Senta.)

The postlude of Daland's aria must be played in full: during the first four bars Daland turns to leave without further ado; with the fifth and sixth bars he stops and turns round again; the following seven bars accompany his partly pleased, partly curious and expectant gestures as he observes now Senta and now the Dutchman; during the subsequent two bars for the double basses he goes as far as the door, shaking his head; with the resumption of the theme by the wind instruments he puts his head back round the door and once more withdraws it in vexation, closing the door behind him, so that he has completely disappeared by the entry of the F sharp chord for the wind instruments. The remainder of the postlude, together with the *ritornello* of the following duet, is accompanied by complete immobility and utter silence on stage: Senta and the Dutchman are lost in rapt contemplation of each other, from opposite sides of the stage. (The performers need not fear that the situation will bore the audience: it is a matter of experience that this is precisely the moment which most powerfully engrosses the spectator and best prepares him for the following scene.)

The whole succeeding E major section should be executed by the Dutchman with an outward appearance of total calm and dignity, however passionate and moving his words; his hands and arms alone may be used (but only sparingly) to emphasize his stronger emotions.

The Dutchman does not stir until the two bars of the timpani solo, before the following E minor tempo, when he approaches Senta: during the short *ritornello* he moves a few steps towards the middle of the stage with a certain self-consciousness and mournful courtesy. (I must here tell the conductor that experience has shown me that I was mistaken in marking the tempo *un poco meno sostenuto*: the long preceding tempo, admittedly, is somewhat slow at the beginning – particularly in the Dutchman's first solo – but little by little it instinctively brightens towards the close, so that with the entry of the E minor the pace must necessarily be somewhat restrained once more, in order to give at least the opening of this section the feeling of solemn calm it requires. The four-bar phrase, in fact, must be expressed in such a hesitant fashion that the fourth bar is played in strict *ritenuto*: the same thing applies to the first phrase now sung by the Dutchman.) With the ninth and tenth bars, during the timpani solo, the Dutchman takes one, then two steps towards Senta. With the eleventh and twelfth bars, however, the tempo must become somewhat brisker, so that the B minor 'Du könntest dich' etc. ('Could you be mine for ever) expresses the tempo I really meant – *moderato*, certainly, but not quite so dragging – which is to be maintained throughout this section. At the *più animato*, 'So unbedingt, wie' etc. ('What, so unquestioningly'), the Dutchman betrays the deep impression Senta's first words have made on him: he must sing this passage with more visible emotion. However, Senta's passionate cry, 'O, welche Leiden! Könnt' ich Trost dir bringen' ('O, what sorrows! Could I bring you comfort') moves him to the quick: with amazed admiration he softly stammers the words 'Welch' holder Klang im nächtlichen Gewühl' ('How sweet a sound in my night of tumult'). With the *molto più animato* he is scarcely master of himself; he sings with the utmost fire of passion, and with the words 'Allewiger, durch *diese* sei's' ('Eternal One, let it be through *her*') he throws himself to his knees. With the *agitato* (B minor) he rises to his feet impetuously: his love for Senta expresses itself in his terror at the thought of the danger she places herself in by reaching out the hand of salvation to him. He sees it as a hideous crime and, in his passionate protest against her sharing in his fate, he becomes a human being through and through, whereas up until now he has only given us the terrible impression of a ghost. Therefore the performer must give even his outer bearing the expression of human passion: he falls to the ground before Senta with the closing words 'nennst ew'ge Treue du nicht dein' ('keep your vow […] true constancy') as if destroyed, so that Senta stands above him like an angel, as she tells him what she means by eternal loyalty. During the *ritornello* of the succeeding *allegro molto*, the Dutchman raises himself with solemn exaltation: his voice rises to the sublimest heights of victory. In all that follows there can be no more room for misunderstanding: at his last entry, in the third act, all is passion, anguish, despair. I would especially stress that the singer should not drag the recitative passages but should take everything in the most spirited, forceful tempo.

Senta's role will be hard to misinterpret; I should just like to warn against one thing: the dreamy side of her nature must not be portrayed in a modern, sickly, sentimental fashion! In fact, Senta is quite the opposite of this – she is a tough, Nordic girl, and even in her apparent sentimentality she is thoroughly naive. Yet it is precisely such a naive nature which, bred in that characteristically Nordic world, would be most susceptible to impressions, such as that of the Ballad of the Flying Dutchman and the picture of the pale sailor, and most inclined to succumb to the desire to redeem the damned: this takes the form of a powerful monomania in her, which is sometimes to be found in extremely naive natures. It has been noted that Norwegian girls can be moved by such strong emotions that death is caused by the sudden stopping of the heart. Such a 'sickness' is also to be ascribed to the pale Senta.

Nor is Erik to be portrayed as a sentimental whiner: on the contrary, he is stormy, impulsive and sombre, like every man who lives alone (particularly in the northern highlands). His cavatina in the third act should not be rendered in a sickly manner, which would do the role a gross injustice, but must, on the contrary, breathe heartache and melancholy. (Everything that might justify a false conception of this piece, such as its falsetto passage and final cadenza, I implore may be either altered or struck out.)

Furthermore, I entreat the performer of Daland not to drag his role into the realm of comedy: he is a rough and hardy character drawn from life, a sailor who braves storms and dangers in the hope of gain and who in no way regards the sale (for so it must seem) of his daughter to a rich man as disgraceful: he thinks and acts like millions of others, without the least suspicion that he is doing any wrong.

Thematic Guide

Themes from the opera have been identified by the numbers in square brackets in the article on the music. These are also printed at corresponding points in the libretto, so that the words can be related to the musical themes.

Overture

[18] Più vivo

STEERSMAN   Moderato

Mit Ge - wit-ter und Sturm aus fer-nem Meer, mein Mä - del,   bin dir nah'!

[19] Moderato

STEERSMAN

Mein   Mä - del, wenn nicht Süd-wind wär', ich nim-mer wohl käm' zu dir:

a

ach, lie-ber Süd-wind blas' noch mehr!

[20]   *sostenuto*

[21] Allegro molto agitato

[22] Maestoso

DUTCHMAN

Dich fra - ge ich,   ge-pries'-ner En - gel Got - tes,

[23] Molto passionato   [24]   Lento

[25] Animato

[26] Allegretto

GIRLS

Summ' und brumm', du gu-tes Räd - chen,

[27a] Allegro non troppo

SENTA

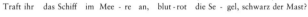

Traft ihr das Schiff im Mee - re an, blut-rot die Se - gel, schwarz der Mast?

[27b]

SENTA

Ach! wann wirst du, blei - cher See - mann, es fin - den?

[28] Prestissimo possibile

MARY

Das Schiffs-volk kommt mit lee - rem Ma-gen.

[29] Allegro appassionato, ma un poco ritenuto

ERIK

Mein Herz, voll Treu - e bis zum Sterb - en

[30]

[31]

timpani

[32] *Aria No. 6*

Allegro moderato

[33] Allegro molto

SENTA

Was   ist's, das mäch - tig in   mir   le - bet,

[34] *Trio*

Allegro vivace

[35] (*Compare* [17])

[Animato, ma non troppo Allegro]

[36]

[37]

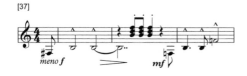

[38]

[39] *No. 8 Finale*

[40] *Cavatina*

Andante **ERIK**

Willst je-nes Tags du nicht mehr dich ent - sin -nen,

Der fliegende Holländer

Note on the Versions

There is still some confusion about whether *Der fliegende Holländer* should be performed in one act or three. While a penniless exile in Paris (1839–42), Wagner was persuaded that, if he turned his existing sketches for *Le Hollandais volant* into a one-act curtain-raiser, there might be some chance of the work being put on at the Opéra, but there was no Paris performance at this time. The premiere production in Dresden in 1843 was given in three acts, and every subsequent production in Wagner's lifetime followed this scheme. He also made revisions to the score in 1844, 1846 and 1852, toning down the weight of the brass and the use of *tremolando* criticised by Berlioz. In 1860 he replaced the original *forte* ending of both the Overture and Act Three with a quiet, transfigured quotation from Senta's Ballad followed by a motif from *Tristan und Isolde*; in the case of the Overture this was preceded by a remarkable passage of *Tristan*-like melodic development and harmonies. In 1864 he started (but never finished) a completely new sketch for the melody of Senta's Ballad, in addition to making minor adjustments to stage directions, libretto and score. Through all these changes, however, the work remained in three acts until, in 1901, Wagner's widow Cosima presented its first staging at Bayreuth. The striking manner in which the music for Acts Two and Three begins precisely where the previous act had finished makes this dovetailing simple to achieve and many subsequent productions and recordings of the work have followed this practice.

THE CHARACTERS

DALAND, *a Norwegian sea captain*   bass
SENTA, *Daland's daughter*   soprano
ERIK, *a hunter*   tenor
MARY, *Senta's nurse*   mezzo-soprano
STEERSMAN   tenor
THE DUTCHMAN   bass-baritone

Norwegian sailors, the Dutchman's crew, women of
the village

The Norwegian coast

Der fliegende Holländer

Romantic opera in three acts
by Richard Wagner

Libretto by the composer

English translation by Lionel Salter

Der fliegende Holländer was first performed at the Royal Saxon Court Theatre, Dresden, on 2nd January 1843. It was first performed in Britain at the Theatre Royal, Drury Lane (in Italian, as *L'Olandese dannato*) on 23rd July 1870. The first performance in the United States, also in Italian, was at the Philadelphia Academy of Music on 8th November 1876.

The German libretto has been laid out in accordance with the one printed in vol. 1 of Wagner's *Gesammelte Schriften und Dichtungen* (Collected Writings) prepared under the composer's supervision and first printed in Leipzig in 1871. The English translation follows the same layout.

Ouvertüre [1–12]

ERSTER AUFZUG

Steiles Felsenufer.

Das Meer nimmt den größeren Teil der Bühne ein; weite Aussicht auf dasselbe. Finsteres Wetter; heftiger Sturm.

Das Schiff Dalands hat soeben dicht am Ufer Anker geworfen: die Matrosen sind mit geräuschvoller Arbeit beschäftigt, die Segel aufzuhissen, Taue auszuwerfen usw. Daland ist an das Land gegangen; er ersteigt einen Felsen und sieht landeinwärts, die Gegend ist zu erkennen.

Nr. 1 Introduktion

MATROSEN *(während der Arbeit)*   [10, 13, 14]
   Hojoje! Hojoje! Hallojo! Ho!

DALAND *(vom Felsen herabkommend)*
   Kein Zweifel! Sieben Meilen fort
   trieb uns der Sturm vom sich'ren Port.
   So nah' dem Ziel nach langer Fahrt
   war mir der Streich noch aufgespart!

STEUERMANN *(von Bord, durch die hohlen Hände rufend)*
   Ho! Kapitän!   [2]

DALAND
               Am Bord bei euch, wie steht's?

STEUERMANN *(wie zuvor)*
   Gut, Kapitän! Wir sind auf sich'rem Grund!

DALAND
   Sandwike ist's! Genau kenn' ich die Bucht.   [15]
   – Verwünscht! Schon sah am Ufer ich mein Haus,   [16]
   Senta, mein Kind, glaubt' ich schon zu umarmen!

Overture [1–12]

ACT ONE

A steep rocky shore.

The sea occupies the greater part of the stage: a wide view over it. Foul weather; a violent storm.

Daland's ship has just cast anchor near the shore; the sailors are noisily occupied in furling the sails, casting ropes, etc. Daland has gone ashore: he climbs a cliff and looks landwards to get his bearings.

No. 1 Introduction

SAILORS *(at work)*   [10, 13, 14]
   Hoyoye! Hoyoye! Halloyo! Ho!

DALAND *(coming down from the cliff)*
   No doubt of it! Seven miles the storm
   has driven us off from safe haven.
   So near our goal after this long voyage
   this trick was saved up for me!

STEERSMAN *(on board, shouting through his cupped hands)*
   Ho! Captain!   [2]

DALAND
            How goes it with you on board?

STEERSMAN *(as before)*
   All's well, Captain! We have firm moorings.

DALAND
   This is Sandvika: I know the bay well.   [15]
   – Damnation! I saw my house on the shore,   [16]
   and thought to embrace Senta, my child!

85

Da bläst es aus dem Teufelsloch heraus...
Wer baut auf Wind, baut auf Satans Erbarmen!

(an Bord gehend)

Was hilft's? Geduld! Der Sturm lässt nach;
wenn so er tobt, währt's nicht lang.

(an Bord)

He, Bursche! Lange wart ihr wach:
zur Ruhe denn! Mir ist nicht bang!

(Die Matrosen steigen in den Schiffsraum.)

Nun, Steuermann, die Wache nimm für mich!
Gefahr ist nicht, doch gut ist's, wenn du wachst.

STEUERMANN
Seid außer Sorg'! Schlaft ruhig, Kapitän!

(Daland geht in die Kajüte. Der Steuermann allein auf dem Verdeck. Der Sturm hat sich etwas gelegt und wiederholt sich nur in abgesetzten Pausen; in hoher See türmen sich die Wellen. Der Steuermann macht noch einmal die Runde, dann setzt er sich am Ruder nieder.)

STEUERMANN *(gähnt, dann rüttelt er sich auf, als ihm der Schlaf ankommt)*

Mit Gewitter und Sturm aus fernem Meer –   [18]
   mein Mädel, bin dir nah'!
Über turmhohe Flut vom Süden her –
   mein Mädel, ich bin da!
Mein Mädel, wenn nicht Südwind wär',   [19]
   ich nimmer wohl käm' zu dir:
ach, lieber Südwind, blas' noch mehr!   [19b]
   Mein Mädel verlangt nach mir!
      Hohoje! Halloho! Jolohohoho!

(Eine Woge schwillt an und rüttelt heftig das Schiff. Der Steuermann fährt auf und sieht nach; er überzeugt sich, dass kein Schade

Then came this blast from the depths of hell...
to rely on the wind is to rely on Satan's mercy!

(going on board)

Ah well! Patience, the storm abates;
so fierce a storm could not last.

(on board)

Hey, my lads! You've kept watch a long time:
now get some rest! There's no more to fear!

(The sailors go below.)

Now, Steersman, will you take the watch for me?
There's no danger, but it'd be better if you kept watch.

STEERSMAN
Think no more of it! Sleep sound, Captain!

(Daland goes into his cabin. The steersman is alone on deck. The storm has somewhat abated and returns only at sporadic intervals: the waves are still rough on the open sea. The steersman makes his round once more, then sits down near the rudder.)

STEERSMAN *(yawns, then rouses himself as sleep comes over him)*

Through thunder and storm, from distant seas   [18]
   I draw near, my lass!
Through towering waves, from the south
   I am here, my lass!
My girl, were there no south wind   [19]
   I could never come to you:
ah, dear south wind, blow once more!   [19b]
   My lass longs for me.
     Hohoye! Halloho! Yolohohoho!

(A wave breaks against the ship, shaking it violently. The steersman starts up and looks around; having satisfied himself that no harm

geschehen, setzt sich wieder und singt, während ihn die Schläfrigkeit
immer mehr übermannt.) [17, 14]

Von des Südens Gestad', aus weitem Land –
ich hab' an dich gedacht;
durch Gewitter und Meer vom Mohrenstrand –
hab' dir was mitgebracht.
Mein Mädel, preis' den Südwind hoch,
ich bring' dir ein gülden Band;
ach, lieber Südwind, blase doch!
Mein Mädel hätt' gern den Tand.
Hohoje! Halloho!

(Er kämpft mit der Müdigkeit und schläft endlich ein.)

(Der Sturm beginnt von neuem heftig zu wüten; es wird finsterer. In
der Ferne zeigt sich das Schiff des „Fliegenden Holländers" mit blut-
roten Segeln und schwarzen Masten. Es naht sich schnell der Küste
nach der dem Schiffe des Norwegers entgegengesetzten Seite [1]; mit
einem furchtbaren Krach sinkt der Anker in den Grund. Der Steu-
ermann Dalands zuckt aus dem Schlafe auf; ohne seine Stellung zu
verlassen, blickt er flüchtig nach dem Steuer, und, überzeugt, dass
kein Schade geschehen, brummt er den Anfang seines Liedes „Mein
Mädel, wenn nicht Südwind wär" und schläft von neuem ein. Stumm
und ohne das geringste Geräusch hisst die gespenstische Mannschaft
des Holländers die Segel auf.) [1, 14, 3, 17, 19]

Nr. 2 Arie [20]

(Der Holländer kommt an das Land. Er trägt schwarze Kleidung.)

HOLLÄNDER
Die Frist ist um, und abermals verstrichen
sind sieben Jahr'. Voll Überdruß wirft mich
das Meer ans Land... Ha, Stolzer Ozean!
In kurzer Frist sollst du mich wieder tragen!
Dein Trotz ist beugsam, doch ewig meine Qual!
– Das Heil, das auf dem Land ich suche, nie
werd' ich es finden! Euch, des Weltmeers Fluten,

has been done, he sits down again and sings, while sleep gradually
overcomes him.)   [17, 14]

On southern shores, in distant lands
   I have thought of you;
through storm and sea, from Moorish strands
   a gift I have brought for you.
My girl, praise the fair south wind,
   for I bring you a golden ring;
ah, dear south wind, then blow!
   My lass would fain have her gift.
      Hohoye! Halloho!

(He struggles with his fatigue and finally falls asleep.)

(The storm begins to rage violently: it grows darker. In the distance
appears the ship of the 'Flying Dutchman', with blood-red sails
and black masts. She rapidly nears the shore, on the side oppo-
site the Norwegian ship [1]; *with a fearful crash she casts anchor.*
Daland's steersman starts up from his sleep; without leaving his
place he glances hastily at the helm and, reassured that no harm
has been done, murmurs the beginning of his song 'My girl, were
there no south wind', and falls asleep again. Silently, and without
the slightest sound, the spectral crew of the Dutchman furl the sails.)
[1, 14, 3, 17, 19]

No. 2 Aria   [20]

(The Dutchman comes ashore, wearing black clothing.)

DUTCHMAN
   The time is up, and once again seven years
   have elapsed. The sea, sated, casts me
   upon land... Ha! Haughty ocean!
   Shortly you must bear me again!
   Your stubbornness can be changed, but my doom is eternal!
   Never shall I find the redemption I seek on land!
   To you, surging ocean, I remain true

bleib' ich getreu, bis eure letzte Welle
sich bricht, und euer letztes Nass versiegt!
   – Wie oft in Meeres tiefsten Schlund   [21]
stürzt' ich voll Sehnsucht mich hinab:
doch ach! den Tod, ich fand ihn nicht!   [6]
Da, wo der Schiffe furchtbar Grab,
trieb *mein* Schiff ich zum Klippengrund:
doch ach! mein Grab, es schloss sich nicht!
Verhöhnend droht' ich dem Piraten,
in wildem Kampfe erhofft ich Tod:
„Hier" – rief ich – „zeige deine Taten!
Von Schätzen voll ist Schiff und Boot."   [1]
Doch ach! des Meer's barbar'scher Sohn
schlägt bang das Kreuz und flieht davon.
    – Wie oft in Meeres tiefsten Schlund
stürzt' ich voll Sehnsucht mich hinab.
Da, wo der Schiffe furchtbar Grab
trieb mein Schiff ich im Klippengrund:
Nirgends ein Grab! Niemals der Tod!
Dies der Verdammnis Schreckgebot.
Dich frage ich, gepries'ner Engel Gottes,   [22]
der meines Heils Bedingung mir gewann;
war ich Unsel'ger Spielwerk deines Spottes,
als die Erlösung du mir zeigtest an?
Vergeb'ne Hoffnung! Furchtbar, eitler Wahn!   [20]
Un ew'ge Treu' auf Erden – ist's getan!
    Nur *eine* Hoffnung soll mir bleiben,   [23]
    nur *eine* unerschüttert steh'n:
    so lang' der Erde Keime treiben,
    so muss sie doch zugrunde geh'n.
    Tag des Gerichtes! Jüngster Tag!
    Wann brichst du an in meine Nacht?
    Wann dröhnt er, der Vernichtungsschlag,
    mit dem die Welt zusammenkracht?
    Wann alle Toten aufersteh'n,   [23]
    dann werde ich in Nichts vergeh'n.

until your last wave breaks
and your last waters run dry!
  – How often into ocean's deepest maw   [21]
  I have plunged longingly;
    but alas! I have not found death!   [6]
  There, on the reefs, fearful graveyard
  of ships, I have driven *my* ship;
  but ah! the grave would not take me!
  Mocking, I challenged the pirate
  and hoped for death in fierce affray:
  'Here,' I cried, 'prove your deeds!
  My ship is filled with treasure.'   [1]
  But ah! the sea's barbarous son
  crossed himself in fear, and fled.
  – How often into ocean's deepest maw
  I have plunged longingly.
  There on the reefs, fearful graveyard
  of ships, I have driven my ship:
  nowhere a grave! Death never comes!
  This is the dread sentence of damnation.
I ask thee, blessed angel from heaven,   [22]
who won for me the terms for my absolution:
was I the unhappy butt of thy mockery
when thou didst show me the way of release?
Vain hope! Dread, empty delusion!   [20]
Constant faith on earth is a thing of the past!
  One *single* hope shall remain with me,   [23]
  it *alone* shall stand unshaken:
  long though the earth may put out new shoots,
  it yet must perish.
  Day of Judgement! Day of doom!
  When will you dawn and end my night?
  When will the blow of annihilation resound,
  which shall crack the world asunder?
  When all the dead rise again,   [23]
  then shall I pass into the void.

91

Ihr Welten, endet euren Lauf!

Ew'ge Vernichtung, nimm mich auf! [1]

MANNSCHAFT DES HOLLÄNDERS *(aus dem Schiffsraum)*

Ew'ge Vernichtung, nimm uns auf! [1]

Nr. 3 Szene, Duett und Chor

(Daland erscheint auf dem Verdeck seines Schiffes [17]; er sieht sich nach dem Winde um und erblickt das Schiff des Holländers, nach dem Steuermann sich umsehend.)

DALAND

He! Holla! Steuermann!

STEUERMANN *(sich schlaftrunken halb aufrichtend)*
                  's ist nichts! 's ist nichts!

(Um seine Munterkeit zu bezeugen, nimmt er sein Lied auf.)

Ach, lieber Südwind, blas' noch mehr, [19a]
    mein Mädel...

DALAND *(ihn heftig aufrüttelnd)*

Du siehst nichts? Gelt, du wachest brav, mein Bursch!

Dort liegt ein Schiff... wie lange schliefst du schon?

STEUERMANN *(rasch auffahrend)*

Zum Teufel auch! Verzeiht mir, Kapitän!

(Er setzt hastig das Sprachrohr an und ruft der Mannschaft des Holländers zu.)

Wer da?

(Pause. Keine Antwort.)

            Wer da?

(Pause)

You stars above, cease your course!
Eternal extinction, fall on me!   [1]

THE DUTCHMAN'S CREW *(from the ship's hold)*
Eternal extinction, fall on us!   [1]

No. 3 Scene, duet and chorus

(Daland appears on the deck of his ship [17]; he takes the direction of the wind and notices the Dutchman's ship, while looking around for the steersman.)

DALAND
Hey! Holla! Steersman!

STEERSMAN *(half rising, still dazed with sleep)*
It's nothing! It's nothing!

(To show his wakefulness, he takes up his song.)

Ah, dear south wind, blow once more;   [19a]
my lass...

DALAND *(shaking him vigorously)*
You see nothing? You keep fine watch, my lad!
There lies a ship... how long have you been asleep?

STEERSMAN *(starting up quickly)*
The Devil take it! Forgive me, Captain!

(He hastily takes up the speaking tube and hails the Dutchman's crew.)

Ahoy there!

(Pause. No reply.)

Ahoy there!

(Pause)

DALAND
                        Es scheint, sie sind gerad'
    so faul als wir.

STEUERMANN *(wie vorher)*
                        Gebt Antwort! Schiff und Flagge?

DALAND *(indem er den Holländer am Lande erblickt)*
    Lass' ab! Mich dünkt, ich seh' den Kapitän!
    He! Holla! Seemann! Nenne dich! Wess' Landes?   [24]

HOLLÄNDER *(nach einer Pause, ohne seine Stellung zu verlassen)*
    Weit komm' ich her: verwehrt bei Sturm und Wetter
    ihr mir den Ankerplatz?

DALAND
                        Verhüt' es Gott!
    Gastfreundschaft kennt der Seemann. – Wer bist du?

HOLLÄNDER
    Holländer.

DALAND *(ist ans Land gekommen)*
                        Gott zum Gruß! – So trieb auch dich
    der Sturm an diesen nackten Felsenstrand?
    Mir ging's nicht besser: wenig Meilen nur
    von hier ist meine Heimat; fast erreicht,
    musst' ich aufs neu' mich von ihr wenden. Sag',
    woher kommst du? Hast Schaden du genommen?

HOLLÄNDER
    Mein Schiff ist fest, es leidet keinen Schaden.   [24]
        Durch Sturm und bösen Wind verschlagen,
        irr' auf den Wassern ich umher –
    wie lange, weiß ich kaum zu sagen:
    schon zähl' ich nicht die Jahre mehr.
    Unmöglich dünkt mich's, dass ich nenne
    die Länder alle, die ich fand:
    das eine nur, nach dem ich brenne,

DALAND

It seems they're just

as idle as we are.

STEERSMAN

Give answer! What ship, and what flag?

DALAND *(who has meanwhile noticed the Dutchman ashore)*
Let be! I think I see the captain.
Hey! Holla! Seaman! What is your name and country?   [24]

DUTCHMAN *(after a pause, without changing his position)*
Far have I come: in storm and tempest
would you deny me anchorage?

DALAND

God forbid! Sailors know the need

for hospitality. Who are you?

DUTCHMAN
A Dutchman.

DALAND *(going ashore)*

God give you greeting! So the storm

drove you too on this barren rocky shore?
I fared no better: my home
is but a few miles from here;
nearly there, I had to turn away again. Tell me,
where do you come from? Have you suffered damage?

DUTCHMAN

My ship is safe and took no damage.   [24]
    Driven on by storms and violent winds,
    I have wandered over the oceans –
for how long I can scarcely say:
I no longer count the years.
It's impossible, I think, to name
all the countries where I've been;
the only one for which I yearn

95

ich find' es nicht, mein Heimatland!
Vergönne mir auf kurze Frist dein Haus,   [24]
und deine Freundschaft soll dich nicht gereu'n.
Mit Schätzen aller Gegenden und Zonen
ist reich mein Schiff beladen, willst du handeln,
so sollst du sicher deines Vorteils sein.

DALAND
Wie wunderbar! Soll deinem Wort ich glauben?
Ein Unstern, scheint's, hat dich bis jetzt verfolgt.
Um dir zu frommen, biet' ich, was ich kann:
doch – darf ich fragen, was dein Schiff enthält?

HOLLÄNDER *(gibt seiner Mannschaft ein Zeichen; zwei von
derselben bringen eine Kiste ans Land)*
Die seltensten der Schätze sollst du seh'n,
kostbare Perlen, edelstes Gestein.

(Er öffnet die Kiste.)

Blick' hin, und überzeuge dich vom Werte
des Preises, den ich für ein gastlich' Dach
dir biete.

DALAND *(voll Erstaunen den Inhalt der Kiste prüfend)*
Wie? Ist's möglich? Diese Schätze!
Wer ist so reich, den Preis dafür zu bieten?

HOLLÄNDER
Den Preis? Soeben hab' ich ihn genannt:
dies für das Obdach einer einz'gen Nacht!
Doch, was du siehst, ist nur der kleinste Teil
von dem, was meines Schiffes Raum verschließt.
Was frommt der Schatz? Ich habe weder Weib   [24]
noch Kind, und meine Heimat find' ich nie!
All' meinen Reichtum biet' ich dir, wenn bei
den Deinen du mir neue Heimat gibst.

I never find, my homeland!
Grant me the shelter of your house awhile, [24]
and you will not regret your friendship.
With treasures from every region and zone
my ship is richly laden; if you will bargain,
you will certainly be the gainer.

DALAND
How amazing! Can I believe your words?
An unlucky star, it seems, has dogged you till now.
I offer whatever I can do to be of service:
but may I ask what your ship contains?

DUTCHMAN *(making a sign to his crew, two of whom bring a chest ashore)*
You shall see the rarest of treasures,
precious pearls, costly gems.

(He opens the chest.)

Look here, and convince yourself of the value
of what I offer you for your friendly roof.

DALAND *(looking at the contents of the chest in utter astonishment)*
What? Is it possible? This treasure?
Who is rich enough to offer a price for it?

DUTCHMAN
The price? I have just named it:
this for lodging for a single night!
Yet what you see is but a fraction
of what is stored in my ship's hold.
What good is wealth to me? I have neither wife [24]
nor child, and can never find my native land!
All my riches I offer you, if you
give me a home with you and yours.

DALAND
Was muss ich hören!

HOLLÄNDER
Hast du eine Tochter?

DALAND
Fürwahr, ein treues Kind.

HOLLÄNDER
Sie sei mein Weib!

DALAND *(freudig betroffen)*
Wie? Hör ich recht? Meine Tochter sein Weib?
Er selbst spricht aus den Gedanken...
Fast fürcht' ich, wenn unentschlossen ich bleib',
er müsst' im Vorsatze wanken.
Wüsst ich, ob ich wach' oder träume!
Kann ein Eidam willkommener sein?
Ein Tor, wenn das Glück ich versäume!
Voll Entzücken schlage ich ein.

HOLLÄNDER
Ach, ohne Weib, ohne Kind bin ich,
nichts fesselt mich an die Erde!
Rastlos verfolgt das Schicksal mich,
die Qual nur war mir Gefährte.
Nie werd' ich die Heimat erreichen:
zu was frommt mir der Güter Gewinn?
Lässt du zu dem Bund dich erweichen,
oh! so nimm meine Schätze dahin!

DALAND
Wohl, Fremdling, hab' ich eine schöne Tochter,   [25]
mit treuer Kindeslieb' ergeben mir;
sie ist mein Stolz, das höchste meiner Güter,
mein Trost im Unglück, meine Freud' im Glück.

DALAND
What do I hear?

DUTCHMAN
Have you a daughter?

DALAND
Indeed, a loving child.

DUTCHMAN
Let her be my wife!

DALAND *(joyfully taken aback)*
What? Do I hear aright? My daughter his wife?
He seems to mean what he says…
I'm half afraid, if I remain wavering,
he will change his mind.
If I only knew if I were awake or dreaming!
Could there be a more welcome son-in-law?
I'd be a fool to let this fortune slip!
With delight I agree.

DUTCHMAN
Ah, I have no wife or child,
nothing to bind me to this earth!
Fate pursues me relentlessly,
with torment as my only companion.
Never shall I reach my home:
what avails the wealth I've won?
If you will consent to this tie,
oh, then take my treasure for your own!

DALAND
Indeed, stranger, I have a fair daughter,   [25]
devoted to me in true filial love;
she is my pride, my most precious possession,
my comfort in sorrow, my joy in happiness.

HOLLÄNDER

Dem Vater stets bewahr' sie ihre Liebe!
ihm treu, wird sie auch treu dem Gatten sein.

DALAND

Du gibst Juwelen, unschätzbare Perlen,
das höchste Kleinod doch, ein treues Weib –

HOLLÄNDER

Du gibst es mir?

DALAND

Ich gebe dir mein Wort.
Mich rührt dein Los; freigebig, wie du bist,
zeigst Edelmut und hohen Sinn du mir:
den Eidam wünsch' ich so; und wär' dein Gut
auch nicht so reich, wählt' ich doch keinen and'ren.

HOLLÄNDER

Hab' Dank! Werd' ich die Tochter heut' noch seh'n?

DALAND

Der nächste günst'ge Wind bringt uns nach Haus;
du sollst sie seh'n, und wenn sie dir gefällt –

HOLLÄNDER

So ist sie mein…

(für sich)

Wird sie mein Engel sein?
Wenn aus der Qualen Schreckgewalten
die Sehnsucht nach dem Heil mich treibt,
ist mir's erlaubt, mich festzuhalten
an *einer* Hoffnung, die mir bleibt?
Darf ich in jenem Wahn noch schmachten
dass sich ein Engel mir erweicht?
Der Qualen, die mein Haupt umnachten,
ersehntes Ziel hätt' ich erreicht?

100

DUTCHMAN
May she always keep her love for her father;
if true to him, she will be true to her husband too.

DALAND
You give jewels, priceless pearls,
yet the greatest of treasures, a faithful wife...

DUTCHMAN
You give to me?

DALAND
                    I give you my word.
Your lot moves me; your liberality
indicates a generous and noble heart to me:
I've wanted such a son-in-law; even were your wealth
not so great, I would choose no other.

DUTCHMAN
My thanks! Shall I see your daughter today?

DALAND
The next favourable wind will bring us home:
you shall see her, and if she pleases you...

DUTCHMAN
She shall be mine...

(aside)

                    Will she be my angel?
If, in the fearful violence of my torment,
longing urges me towards redemption,
am I allowed to cling
to the *one* hope remaining to me?
Dare I cherish the illusion
that an angel will be moved to pity me,
and that, from out the torments which shroud my head,
I have reached my longed-for goal?

Ach, ohne Hoffnung, wie ich bin,
geb' ich der Hoffnung doch mich hin!

DALAND

Gepriesen seid, des Sturms Gewalten,
die ihr an diesen Strand mich triebt!
Fürwahr, bloß brauch' ich festzuhalten,
was sich so schön von selbst mir gibt.
Die ihn an diese Küste brachten,
ihr Winde, sollt gesegnet sein!
Ja, wonach alle Väter trachten,
ein reicher Eidam, er ist mein.
Ja, dem Mann mit Gut und hohem Sinn
geb' froh ich Haus und Tochter hin!

(Der Sturm hat sich gänzlich gelegt; der Wind ist umgeschlagen.)

STEUERMANN *(an Bord)*
Südwind! Südwind!
„Ach, lieber Südwind, blas' noch mehr!"   [19a]

MATROSEN (die Mützen schwenkend)
Halloho! Hohohe! Hallojo!   [13]

DALAND
Du siehst, das Glück ist günstig dir: [17]
der Wind ist gut, die See in Ruh'.
Sogleich die Anker lichten wir
und segeln schnell der Heimat zu.

STEUERMANN und MATROSEN *(die Anker lichtend und die
Segel aufspannend)*
Hoho! Hallojo!

HOLLÄNDER
Darf ich dich bitten, segelst du voran;   [14]
der Wind ist frisch, doch meine Mannschaft müd'.   [7]
Ich gönn' ihr kurze Ruh' und folge dann.

Ah, bereft of hope as I am,
in this hope I still indulge!

DALAND
    I thank the force of the storm
    for driving me onto this strand!
    In truth, I have but to grasp
    what fortune has itself offered me.
    You winds who brought him to these shores,
    blessings upon you!
    Yes, a rich son-in-law,
    which all fathers seek, is mine.
    Yes, to one so wealthy and open-hearted
    I gladly give my house and daughter!

(The storm has completely subsided; the wind has turned round.)

STEERSMAN *(on board)*
    South wind! South wind!
    'Ah, dear south wind, blow once more!'   [19a]

SAILORS *(waving their caps)*
    Halloho! Hohohe! Halloyo!   [13]

DALAND
    You see, fortune favours you: [17]
    the wind is fair, the sea calm.
    Let us weigh anchor forthwith
    and gladly sail for home.

STEERSMAN and SAILORS *(weighing anchor and hoisting sail)*
    Hoho! Halloyo!

DUTCHMAN
    May I ask you to sail on ahead?   [14]
    The wind is fresh, but my crew is weary.   [7]
    I'll let them rest awhile, then follow on.

DALAND
  Doch, unser Wind?

HOLLÄNDER
            Er bläst noch lang' aus Süd!
  Mein Schiff ist schnell, es holt dich sicher ein.

DALAND
  Du glaubst? Wohlan, es möge denn so sein!
  Leb' wohl, mög'st heute du mein Kind noch seh'n!

HOLLÄNDER

                            Gewiss!

DALAND *(an Bord seines Schiffes gehend)*
  Hei! Wie die Segel schon sich bläh'n!
  Hallo! Hallo!

(Er gibt ein Zeichen auf der Schiffspfeife.)

  Frisch, Jungen, greifet an!

MATROSEN *(im Absegeln jubelnd)*
  Mit Gewitter und Sturm aus fernem Meer –   [18]
    mein Mädel, bin dir nah'! Hurra!
  Über turmhohe Flut vom Süden her –
    mein Mädel, ich bin da! Hurra!
  Mein Mädel, wenn nicht Südwind wär',   [19]
    ich nimmer wohl käm' zu dir;
  ach, lieber Südwind, blas' noch mehr!
    Mein Mädel verlangt nach mir.
      Hohoho! Joloho!

(Der Holländer besteigt sein Schiff)   [17, 2, 3, 14]

DALAND
   Yes, but the wind?

DUTCHMAN
                  It's set to blow from the south!
   My ship is swift, and will overtake you.

DALAND
   You think so? Well, so be it!
   Farewell! You may yet see my daughter today!

DUTCHMAN

                              For sure!

DALAND *(going aboard his ship)*
   Hey! How the sails fill out already!
   Ho there! Ho there!

(He gives a signal on his whistle.)

   Quick, lads, cast off!

SAILORS *(exultantly, as they sail away)*
   Through thunder and storm, from distant seas   [18]
      I draw near, my lass! Hurrah!
   Through towering waves, from the south
      I am here, my lass! Hurrah!
   My girl, were there no south wind   [19]
      I could never come to you:
   ah, dear south wind, blow once more!
      My lass longs for me.
         Hohoho! Yoloho!

(The Dutchman goes aboard his ship.)   [17, 2, 3, 14]

ZWEITER AUFZUG

Ein geräumiges Zimmer im Hause Dalands.

An den Seitenwänden Abbildungen von Seegegenständen, Karten usw. An der Wand im Hintergrunde das Bild eines bleichen Mannes mit dunklem Barte und in schwarzer Kleidung.

Mary und die Mädchen sitzen um den Kamin herum und spinnen; Senta, in einem Großvaterstuhl zurückgelehnt und mit unterge- schlagenen Armen, ist im träumerischen Anschauen des Bildes im Hintergrunde versunken.

Nr. 4 Szene, Lied und Ballade

MÄDCHEN

 Summ' und brumm', du gutes Rädchen,   [26]
 munter, munter, dreh' dich um!
 Spinne, spinne tausend Fädchen,
 gutes Rädchen, summ' und brumm'!
Mein Schatz ist auf dem Meere draus',
  er denkt nach Haus
  ans fromme Kind;
mein gutes Rädchen, braus' und saus'!
  Ach! gäbst du Wind,
  er käm' geschwind.
   Spinnt! Spinnt!
  Fleißig, Mädchen!
   Brumm'! Summ'!
  Gutes Rädchen!

MARY

 Ei! Fleißig, fleißig! Wie sie spinnen!
 Will jede sich den Schatz gewinnen.

106

ACT TWO

A spacious room in Daland's house.

On the side walls pictures of sea subjects, maps, etc. On the rear wall the picture of a pale man with a dark beard and in black clothes.

Mary and the girls are seated round the hearth, spinning. Senta leans back in a high-backed armchair, her arms folded, sunk in dreamy contemplation of the portrait in the background.

No. 4 Scene, song and ballad

GIRLS

> Whir and whirl, good wheel,   [26]
> gaily, gaily turn!
> Spin, spin a thousand threads,
> good wheel, whir and whirl!
> My love is out there on the seas,
>> thinking of his dear
>> at home;
> good wheel, roll and roar!
>> Ah, if you could raise a wind,
>> he'd soon be here.
>> Spin, girls,
> spin busily!
>> Whir and whirl,
> good wheel!

MARY

> Ah, busily, how busily they spin!
> Every girl wants to gain a lover.

MÄDCHEN

Frau Mary, still! Denn wohl Ihr wisst,
das Lied noch nicht zu Ende ist.

MARY

So singt! Dem Rädchen lässt's nicht Ruh'. –
Du aber, Senta, schweigst dazu?

MÄDCHEN

Summ' und brumm', du gutes Rädchen,
munter, munter dreh' dich um!
Spinne, spinne tausend Fädchen,
gutes Rädchen, summ' und brumm'!
Mein Schatz da draußen auf dem Meer,
im Süden er
viel Gold gewinnt;
ach, gutes Rädchen, saus' noch mehr!
Er gibt's dem Kind,
wenn's fleißig spinnt.
Spinnt! Spinnt!
Fleißig, Mädchen!
Brumm'! Summ'!
Gutes Rädchen!

MARY *(zu Senta)*

Du böses Kind, wenn du nicht spinnst,
vom Schatz du kein Geschenk gewinnst.

MÄDCHEN

Sie hat's nicht not, dass sie sich eilt;
ihr Schatz nicht auf dem Meere weilt.
Bringt er nicht Gold, bringt er doch Wild –
man weiß ja, was ein Jäger gilt!

(Sie lachen.)

(Senta, ohne ihre Stellung zu verlassen, singt leise einen Vers aus der folgenden Ballade vor sich hin.) [5]

GIRLS

> Dame Mary, hush! For well you know
> Our song is not yet done.

MARY

> Sing then! Let your wheels not rest. –
> But Senta, why are you silent?

GIRLS

> Whir and whirl, good wheel,
> gaily, gaily turn!
> Spin, spin a thousand threads,
> good wheel, whir and whirl!
> My love out on the seas
>> will earn much gold
>> in southern lands;
> ah, good wheel, roar more!
>> He'll give it to his dear
>> if she spins busily.
>>> Spin, girls,
>> spin busily!
>>> Whir and whirl,
>> good wheel!

MARY *(to Senta)*

> You idle girl! If you don't spin,
> you'll get no present from your lad.

GIRLS

> She has no need to hurry;
> her lover does not sail the sea.
> He brings not gold but game –
> we know a hunter's worth!

(They laugh.)

(Without changing her position, Senta softly sings to herself a snatch of the ballad which follows.) [5]

109

MARY

Da seht ihr's! Immer vor dem Bild!
Willst du dein ganzes junges Leben
verträumen vor dem Konterfei?

SENTA *(wie oben)*

Was hast du Kunde mir gegeben,
was mir erzählet, wer er sei?

(seufzend)

Der arme Mann!

MARY

Gott sei mit dir!

MÄDCHEN

Ei, ei! Ei, ei! Was hören wir!
Sie seufzet um den bleichen Mann!

MARY

Den Kopf verliert sie noch darum.

MÄDCHEN

Da sieht man, was ein Bild doch kann!

MARY

Nichts hilft es, wenn ich täglich brumm'!
Komm! Senta! Wend' dich doch herum!

MÄDCHEN

Sie hört Euch nicht – sie ist verliebt.
Ei, ei! Wenn's nur nicht Händel gibt.
Denn Erik hat gar heißes Blut –
dass er nur keinen Schaden tut!
Sagt nichts! Er schießt sonst, wutentbrannt,
den Nebenbuhler von der Wand.

(Sie lachen.)

MARY

You see her! Always before that picture!
Will you dream away your whole youth
in front of that likeness?

SENTA

Why did you tell me,
why did you relate to me, who he was?

(sighing)

Poor man!

MARY

God help you!

GIRLS

Ay, ay! Ay, ay! What do we hear?
She's sighing for that pallid man!

MARY

She's losing her head over him!

GIRLS

You see what a picture can do!

MARY

In vain do I chide her every day.
Come, Senta! Turn round this way!

GIRLS

She doesn't hear you – she's in love!
Ay, ay! If only it doesn't lead to trouble,
for Erik is hot-blooded –
let him do no damage!
Say nothing! Or else in a rage
he'll shoot his rival off the wall.

(They laugh.)

SENTA *(heftig auffahrend)*
O schweigt! Mit eurem tollen Lachen
wollt ihr mich ernstlich böse machen?

MÄDCHEN *(fallen mit komischem Eifer sehr stark ein, indem sie
die Spinnräder heftig und mit großen Geräusche drehen, gleichsam,
um Senta nicht Zeit zum Schmälen zu lassen)*
Summ' und brumm'! Du gutes Rädchen,   [26]
munter, munter dreh' dich um!
Spinne, spinne tausend Fädchen,
gutes Rädchen, summ' und brumm'!

SENTA *(ärgerlich unterbrechend)*
O, macht dem dummen Lied ein Ende,
es brummt und summt nur vor dem Ohr!
Wollt ihr, dass ich mich zu euch wende,
so sucht, was Besseres hervor!

MÄDCHEN
Gut, singe du!

SENTA
                        Hört, was ich rate:
Frau Mary singt uns die Ballade.

MARY
Bewahre Gott! Das fehlte mir!
Den fliegenden Holländer lasst in Ruh'!   [1]

SENTA
Wie oft doch hört' ich sie von dir!
Ich sing' sie selbst; hört, Mädchen, zu!
Lasst mich's euch recht zum Herzen führen,
des Ärmsten Los, es muss euch rühren!

MÄDCHEN
Uns ist es recht.

SENTA
                        Merkt auf die Wort'.

SENTA *(starting up angrily)*
    Be quiet! Would you make me really angry
    with your foolish laughter?

GIRLS *(interrupting her noisily with comic fervour, meanwhile
turning their spinning wheels violently and very loudly as if to give
Senta no opportunity of scolding them)*
    Whir and whirl! Good wheel,   [26]
    gaily, gaily turn!
    Spin, spin a thousand threads,
    good wheel, whir and whirl!

SENTA *(jumping up angrily)*
    O, have done with your stupid song,
    your whirring and whirling wearies my ears!
    If you want me to turn towards you,
    search out something better!

GIRLS
    Well, you sing yourself!

SENTA
                  Hear what I suggest:
    Dame Mary shall sing us the ballad.

MARY
    God forbid! I can't do it!
    Leave the flying Dutchman in peace!   [1]

SENTA
    Yet how often have I heard it from you!
    I'll sing it myself: listen, girls!
    If you will open your hearts to my tale,
    the wretch's lot will surely move you!

GIRLS
    We agree.

SENTA
             Mark what I say!

MÄDCHEN
Dem Spinnrad Ruh'!

MARY *(ärgerlich)*
Ich spinne fort.

(Die Mädchen rücken, nachdem sie ihre Spinnräder beiseite gesetzt haben, die Sitze dem Großvaterstuhle näher und gruppieren sich um Senta. Mary bleibt am Kamin sitzen und spinnt fort.)

SENTA *(im Großvaterstuhl)*
Johohoe! Johohohoe! Johohoe! Johoe!   [1]
Traft ihr das Schiff im Meere an,   [27]
blutrot die Segel, schwarz der Mast?
Auf hohem Bord der bleiche Mann,
des Schiffes Herr, wacht ohne Rast.
Hui! – Wie saust der Wind! – Johohe!   [3, 15, 7]
Hui! – Wie pfeift's im Tau! – Johohe!
Hui! – Wie ein Pfeil fliegt er hin,
ohne Ziel, ohne Rast, ohne Ruh'! –   [4]
Doch kann dem bleichen Manne Erlösung einstens noch werden, [5]
fänd' er ein Weib, das bis in den Tod getreu ihm auf Erden! –
Ach! Wann wirst du, bleicher Seemann, es finden?
Betet zum Himmel, dass bald
ein Weib Treue ihm halt'!

(Gegen das Ende der Strophe kehrt Senta sich gegen das Bild. Die Mädchen hören teilnahmsvoll zu; Mary hat aufgehört zu spinnen.)   [1]

Bei bösem Wind und Sturmes Wut   [27]
umsegeln wollt' er einst ein Kap;
er schwur und flucht' mit tollem Mut:
„In Ewigkeit lass' ich nicht ab!"
Hui! – Und Satan hört's! – Johohe!   [3, 15, 7]
Hui! – Nahm ihm beim Wort! – Johohe!
Hui! – Und verdammt zieht er nun
durch das Meer ohne Rast, ohne Ruh'! –   [4]
Doch, dass der arme Mann noch Erlösung fände auf Erden, [5]
zeigt' Gottes Engel an, wie sein Heil ihm einst könne werden!

GIRLS
 Stop the wheels!

MARY *(angrily)*
 I'll spin on!

(Having put their spinning wheels aside, the girls move their seats nearer to the armchair and group themselves around Senta. Mary remains sitting by the hearth and continues her spinning.)

SENTA *(in the armchair)*
 Yohohoe! Yohohohoe! Yohohoe! Yohoe!   [1]
 Have you seen the ship upon the ocean   [27]
 with blood-red sails and black masts?
 On her bridge a pallid man,
 the ship's master, watches incessantly.
 Whee! How the wind howls! Yohohe!   [3, 15, 7]
 Whee! How it whistles in the rigging! Yohohe!
 Whee! Like an arrow he flies on,
 without aim, without end, without rest!   [4]
 Yet there could be redemption one day for that pale man   [5]
 if he found a wife on earth who'd be true to him till death!
 Ah, when, pale seaman, will you find her?
 Pray Heaven, that soon
 a wife will keep faith with him!

(Towards the end of the stanza Senta turns to the picture. The girls listen attentively; Mary has stopped spinning.)   [1]

 In raging wind and violent storm   [27]
 he once sought to round a cape;
 he cursed, and in a fit of madness swore,
 'In all eternity I'll not give up!'
 Whee! And Satan heard! Yohohe!   [3, 15, 7]
 Whee! Took him at his word! Yohohe!
 Whee! And now, accursed, he roams
 the seas without end, without rest!   [4]
 Yet, so that the poor man still could find redemption on earth, [5]
 God's angel showed him the path to salvation!

SENTA und MÄDCHEN
>Ach! könntest du, bleicher Seemann, es finden!
>>Betet zum Himmel, dass bald
>>ein Weib Treue ihm halt'!

(Die Mädchen sind ergriffen und singen den Schlussreim leise mit. Senta, die schon bei der zweiten Strophe von Stuhle aufgestanden war, fährt mit immer zunehmender Aufregung fort.) [1]

SENTA
>Vor Anker alle sieben Jahr', [27]
>ein Weib zu frei'n, geht er ans Land: –
>er freite alle sieben Jahr',
>noch nie ein treues Weib er fand. –
>Hui! – „Die Segel auf!" – Johohe! [3, 17]
>Hui! – „Den Anker los!" – Johohe!
>Hui! – „Falsche Lieb', falsche Treu'!
>Auf, in See, ohne Rast, ohne Ruh'!" [4]

(Senta, zu heftig angegriffen, sinkt in den Stuhl zurück; die Mädchen singen nach einer Pause leise weiter.)

MÄDCHEN
>Ach, wo weilt sie, die dir Gottes Engel einst könnte zeigen? [5]
>Wo triffst du sie, die bis in den Tod dein bliebe treueigen?

SENTA *(von plötzlicher Begeisterung hingerissen, springt vom Stuhle auf)*
>Ich sei's, die dich durch ihre Treu' erlöse! [12]
>>Mög' Gottes Engel mich dir zeigen!
>>Durch mich sollst du das Heil erreichen!

MARY und MÄDCHEN *(erschreckt aufspringend)*
>Hilf, Himmel! Senta! Senta!

(Erik ist zur Türe hereingetreten und hat Sentas Ausruf vernommen.)

ERIK
>Senta! Senta! Willst du mich verderben?

SENTA and GIRLS
Ah, if you could find it, pallid seaman!
Pray Heaven, that soon
a wife will keep faith with him!

(The girls are deeply moved, and softly sing the final lines with her. Senta, who already at the second stanza had risen from her chair, continues with ever-increasing agitation.) [1]

SENTA
At anchor every seventh year, [27]
he goes ashore to seek a wife.
Every seventh year he's wooed,
but never found a faithful wife.
Whee! 'Unfurl sail!' Yohohe! [3, 17]
Whee! 'Up anchor!' Yohohe!
Whee! 'Faithless love, faithless troth!
Off to sea, without end, without rest!' [4]

(Senta, overcome by her emotion, sinks back in her chair; the girls, after a pause, continue the song softly.)

GIRLS
Ah! Where dwells the maid whom God's angel once predicted? [5]
Where will you meet the one who'll be true to you till death?

SENTA *(seized with a sudden inspiration, springs up from her chair)*
Let me be the one whose loyalty shall save you! [12]
May God's angel reveal me to you!
Through me shall you attain redemption!

MARY and GIRLS *(starting up in terror)*
Heaven help us! Senta, Senta!

(Erik has entered by the door and has heard Senta's outcry.)

ERIK
Senta! Senta! Would you destroy me?

117

MÄDCHEN
Helft, Erik, uns! Sie ist von Sinnen!

MARY
Ich fühl' in mir das Blut gerinnen!
Abscheulich Bild, du sollst hinaus,
kommt nur der Vater erst nach Haus!

ERIK *(düster)*
Der Vater kommt!

SENTA *(die in ihrer letzten Stellung verblieben und von allem nichts*
vernommen hatte, wie erwachend und freudig auffahrend)
Der Vater kommt?

ERIK
Vom Felsen sah sein Schiff ich nah'n.

MÄDCHEN *(voll Freude)*
Sie sind daheim!

MARY *(außer sich, in großer Geschäftigkeit)*
Nun seht, zu was eu'r Treiben frommt!
Im Hause ist noch nichts getan.

MÄDCHEN
Sie sind daheim! Auf, eilt hinaus!

MARY *(die Mädchen zurückhaltend)*
Halt, halt! Ihr bleibet fein im Haus!
Das Schiffsvolk kommt mit leerem Magen.   [28]
In Küch' und Keller! Säumet nicht!
Lasst euch nur von der Neugier plagen –
vor allem geht an eure Pflicht!

MÄDCHEN *(für sich)*
Ach! Wie viel hab' ich ihn zu fragen!
Ich halte mich vor Neugier nicht.
Schon gut! Sobald nur aufgetragen,
hält hier aus länger keine Pflicht.

118

GIRLS
    Erik, help us! She's out of her mind!

MARY
    I feel the blood within me curdle!
    Hateful picture, out you shall go,
    as soon as her father returns!

ERIK *(gloomily)*
    Her father is coming!

SENTA *(who has remained where she was, oblivious of everything, starts up joyfully, as if awaking)*
                    Father is coming?

ERIK
    From the cliff I saw his ship approaching.

GIRLS
    They're home!

MARY *(beside herself, bustling about)*
    Now see what use your work was!
    Nothing in the house is done.

GIRLS
    They're home! Hurry, let's away!

MARY *(detaining the girls)*
    Stop, stop. Stay where you are!
    The sailors will come with empty stomachs.   [28]
    Into the kitchen and cellar, without delay!
    Restrain your curiosity awhile –
    first of all to your tasks!

GIRLS *(aside)*
    Ah, how much I have to ask him!
    I can't restrain my curiosity.
    Enough! As soon as they're fed,
    no task will keep me here longer.

119

(Mary treibt de Mädchen hinaus und folgt ihnen. Senta will ebenfalls gehen; Erik hält sie zurück.)

Nr. 5 Duett

ERIK

Bleib', Senta! Bleib' nur einen Augenblick!
Aus meinen Qualen reiße mich! Doch willst du,
ach! so verdirb mich ganz!

SENTA *(zögernd)*

Was ist... ? Was soll?

ERIK

O Senta, sprich, was aus mir werden soll?
Dein Vater kommt: eh' wieder er verreist,
wird er vollbringen, was schon oft er wollte...

SENTA

Und was meinst du?

ERIK

Dir einen Gatten geben!
Mein Herz, voll Treue bis zum Sterben,   [29]
mein dürftig Gut, mein Jägerglück –
darf so um deine Hand ich werben?
Stößt mich dein Vater nicht zurück?
Wenn dann mein Herz im Jammer bricht,
sag', Senta, wer dann für mich spricht?

SENTA

Ach, schweige, Erik, jetzt! Lass mich hinaus,
den Vater zu begrüßen!
Wenn nicht, wie sonst, an Bord die Tochter kommt,
wird er nicht zürnen müssen?

ERIK

Du willst mich flieh'n?

(Mary drives the girls out and follows them. Senta is also about to leave; Erik detains her.)

No. 5 Duet

ERIK

Stay, Senta! Stay for one moment!
Free me from my torment! Or if you will,
ah, destroy me utterly!

SENTA *(hesitantly)*

What is to be?

ERIK

O Senta, say, what is to become of me?
Your father is coming: before he sets off again
he will bring about what he has often intended...

SENTA

What do you mean?

ERIK

To give you a husband.
My heart, faithful until death,   [29]
my meagre possessions, my skill as a hunter –
can I sue with these for your hand?
Would your father not reject me?
Then, if my heart breaks in anguish,
say, Senta, who will speak for me?

SENTA

Ah, Erik, no more now!
Let me go and greet my father!
If his daughter does not come aboard, as usual,
is he not bound to be vexed?

ERIK

You would fly from me?

121

SENTA

Ich muss zum Port.

ERIK

Du weichst mir aus?

SENTA

Ach, lass mich fort!

ERIK

Fliehst du zurück vor dieser Wunde,   [29]
die du mir schlugst, dem Liebeswahn?
Ach, höre mich zu dieser Stunde,
hör' meine letzte Frage an:
Wenn dieses Herz im Jammer bricht,
wird's Senta sein, die für mich spricht?

SENTA (*schwankend*)

Wie? Zweifelst du an meinem Herzen?
Du zweifelst, ob ich gut dir bin?
O sag', was weckt dir solche Schmerzen?
Was trübt mit Argwohn deinen Sinn?

ERIK

Dein Vater, ach! – nach Schätzen geizt er nur…
Und Senta, du? Wie dürft' auf dich zu zählen?
Erfülltest du nur *eine* meiner Bitten?
Kränkst du mein Herz nicht jeden Tag?

SENTA

Dein Herz?

ERIK

Was soll ich denken? – Jenes Bild…

SENTA

Das Bild?

ERIK

Lässt du von deiner Schwärmerei wohl ab?

SENTA

I must go to the harbour.

ERIK

You shun me?

SENTA

Ah, let me go!

ERIK

Do you flee from these wounds   [29]
you dealt me, crazed with love?
Ah, hear me at this moment,
listen to my last request:
if this heart breaks in anguish,
will it be Senta who speaks for me?

SENTA *(swaying)*

What? Do you doubt my heart?
You doubt whether I care for you?
O say, what stirs in you such sorrows?
What darkens your mind with such distrust?

ERIK

Your father, ah! – he craves only for wealth...
And you, Senta? How can I count upon you?
Have you granted a *single* plea of mine?
Do you not grieve my heart each day?

SENTA

Your heart?

ERIK

What must I think? – That picture...

SENTA

The picture?

ERIK

Can you not end this infatuation?

SENTA

Kann meinem Blick Teilnahme ich verwehren?

ERIK

Und die Ballade – heut' noch sangst du sie!

SENTA

Ich bin ein Kind und weiß nicht, was ich singe…
O sag', wie? Fürchtest du ein Lied, ein Bild?

ERIK

Du bist so bleich… sag', sollte ich's nicht fürchten?

SENTA

Soll mich des Ärmsten Schreckenslos nicht rühren?

ERIK

Mein Leiden, Senta, rührt es dich nicht mehr?

SENTA

O, prahle nicht! Was kann *dein* Leiden sein?
Kennst jenes Unglücksel'gen Schicksal du?

(Sie führt Erik zum Bilde.)

Fühlst du den Schmerz, den tiefen Gram,
mit dem herab er auf mich sieht?
Ach, was die Ruhe für ewig ihm nahm,
wie schneidend Weh durchs Herz mir zieht!

ERIK

Weh' mir! Es mahnt mich mein unsel'ger Traum!
Gott schütze dich! Satan hat dich umgarnt!   [30]

SENTA

Was schreckt dich so?

ERIK

Senta! Lass dir vertrau'n:
ein Traum ist's! Hör ihn zur Warnung an!

124

SENTA

Can I forbid my eyes to sympathize?

ERIK

And the ballad – you sang it again today!

SENTA

I'm but a child, and know not what I sing...
But say, what is it? Do you fear a song, a picture?

ERIK

You are so pale... say, should I not fear them?

SENTA

Should that poor man's dreadful lot not move me?

ERIK

Senta, does my suffering not move you more?

SENTA

Do not exaggerate! What is *your* suffering?
Do you know the fate of that unhappy man?

(She leads Erik to the picture.)

Do you feel the grief, the deep sorrow
with which he looks down at me?
Ah, how that which deprived him of peace for ever
sends a pang of woe through my heart!

ERIK

Alas! I recall my unhappy dream!
God protect you! Satan has you in his snare!   [30]

SENTA

What appals you so?

ERIK

Senta! Let me confide in you:
it is a dream! Listen to its warning!

(Senta setzt sich erschöpft in den Lehnstuhl nieder; bei dem Beginn von Eriks Erzählung versinkt sie wie in magnetischen Schlaf, so dass es scheint, als träume sie den von ihm erzählten Traum ebenfalls. Erik steht an den Stuhl gelehnt zur Seite.)

ERIK *(mit gedämpfter Stimme)*
 Auf hohem Felsen lag' ich träumend,
 sah unter mir des Meeres Flut;
 die Brandung hört' ich, wie sich schäumend
 am Ufer brach der Wogen Wut.
 Ein fremdes Schiff am nahen Strande
 erblickt' ich, seltsam, wunderbar;   [1]
 zwei Männer nahten sich dem Lande,
 der ein', ich sah's, dein Vater war.

SENTA *(mit geschlossenen Augen)*
 Der and're?

ERIK
    Wohl erkannt' ich ihn:
 mit schwarzem Wams, die bleiche Mien'…

SENTA
 Der düst're Blick…

ERIK *(auf das Bild deutend)*
     Der Seemann, er.

SENTA
 Und ich?

ERIK
    Du kamst vom Hause her,
 du flogst, den Vater zu begrüßen;
 doch kaum noch sah ich an dich langen,
 du stürztest zu des Fremden Füßen –   [1]
 ich sah dich seine Knie umfangen…

SENTA *(mit steigender Spannung)*
 Er hub mich auf…

(Senta, exhausted, sits down in the armchair; at the beginning of Erik's narration she sinks into a magnetic sleep, so that she appears to be dreaming the dream being related to her. Erik stands at her side, leaning against the chair.)

ERIK *(in a muffled voice)*
I lay dreaming on the lofty cliff
and watched the surging sea below me;
I heard the breakers, as the force of the waves
dashed them, foaming, against the beach.
I perceived a foreign ship off shore,
strange and mysterious;   [1]
two men were approaching on the shore,
of whom one, I saw, was your father.

SENTA *(with closed eyes)*
The other?

ERIK
           I knew him well:
his black attire, his ashen features...

SENTA
His melancholy eyes...

ERIK *(pointing to the picture)*
           That seaman there.

SENTA
And I?

ERIK
           You came out of the house
and flew to greet your father;
but scarcely did I see you reach him
than you threw yourself at the stranger's feet –   [1]
I saw you clasp his knees...

SENTA *(with growing excitement)*
He raised me up...

127

ERIK
>   An seine Brust;
voll Inbrunst hingst du dich an ihn –
du küsstest ihn mit heißer Lust –

SENTA
> Und dann?

ERIK *(sie überrascht anblickend, nach einer Pause)*
>   Sah ich auf's Meer euch flieh'n.

SENTA *(schnell erwachend, in höchster Verzückung)*
> Er sucht mich auf! Ich muss ihn seh'n! [5]
> Mit ihm muss ich zugrunde geh'n!

ERIK *(in Verzweiflung)*
> Entsetzlich! Ha, mir wird es klar!
> Sie ist dahin! Mein Traum sprach wahr!

(Er stürzt voll Entsetzen ab.) [1]

SENTA *(nach dem Ausbruch ihrer Begeisterung in stummes Sinnen versunken, verbleibt in ihrer Stellung, den Blick auf das Bild geheftet; nach einer Pause singt sie leise, aber tief ergriffen, den Schluss der Ballade)*
> Ach, möchtest du, bleicher Seemann, sie finden! [5b]
>   Betet zum Himmel, dass bald
>   ein Weib Treue ihm… Ha!

(Die Tür geht auf. Daland und der Holländer treten ein. Sentas Blick streift vom Bilde auf den Holländer, sie stößt einen Schrei der Überraschung aus und bleibt wie festgebannt stehen, ohne ihr Auge vom Holländer abzuwenden) [31]

Nr. 6 Finale: Arie, Duett und Terzett

(Der Holländer geht langsam in den Vordergrund.)

DALAND *(nachdem er an der Schwelle stehengeblieben, näher tretend)*
>   Mein Kind, du siehst mich auf der Schwelle…
>   Wie ? Kein Umarmen? Keinen Kuss?

ERIK
                    Upon his breast;
        ardently you clung to him –
        you kissed him in hot longing...

SENTA
        And then?

ERIK *(looking at her in astonishment, after a pause)*
                    I saw you both put to sea.

SENTA *(awaking suddenly, in the utmost rapture)*
        He asks for me! I must see him!   [5]
        With him I must perish!

ERIK *(in distress)*
        Oh, horror! This all becomes clear!
        She is lost to me! My dream told the truth!

(He rushes off in horror.)   [1]

SENTA *(after her outburst of excitement remains where she is, sunk in silent meditation, her eyes fixed on the portrait; after a pause she sings, softly but with deep emotion, the end of the ballad.)*
        Ah! may you find her, pale seaman!   [5b]
            Pray Heaven, that soon
            a wife will keep faith... Ah!

(The door opens. Daland and the Dutchman enter. Senta's gaze sweeps from the portrait to the Dutchman; she cries out in astonishment and remains as if spellbound, without taking her eyes off him.)   [31]

No. 6 Finale: Aria, duet and trio

(The Dutchman comes slowly forward.)

DALAND *(having remained standing at the threshold, comes forward)*
                    My child, you see me at the door...
                    What? No embrace? No kiss?

129

Du bleibst gebannt an deiner Stelle –
verdien' ich, Senta, solchen Gruß?

SENTA *(als Daland bei ihr anlangt, ergreift sie seine Hand)*
Gott dir zum Gruß!

(ihn näher an sich ziehend)

Mein Vater, sprich!
Wer ist der Fremde?

DALAND *(lächelnd)*
Drängst du mich?
Mög'st du, mein Kind, den fremden Mann willkommen heißen? [32]
Seemann ist er, gleich mir, das Gastrecht spricht er an.
Lang' ohne Heimat, stets auf fernen, weiten Reisen,
in fremden Landen er der Schätze viel gewann.
Aus seinem Vaterland verwiesen,
für einen Herd er reichlich lohnt:
sprich, Senta, würd' es dich verdrießen,
wenn dieser Fremde bei uns wohnt?

(Senta nickt beifällig mit dem Kopfe; Daland wendet sich zum Holländer.)

Sagt, hab' ich sie zu viel gepriesen?
Ihr seht sie selbst – ist sie Euch recht?
Soll ich von Lob noch überfließen?
Gesteht, sie zieret ihr Geschlecht!

(Der Holländer macht eine Bewegung des Beifalls.)

Mög'st du, mein Kind, dem Manne freundlich dich erweisen!
Von deinem Herzen auch spricht holde Gab' er an;
reich ihm die Hand, denn Bräutigam sollst du ihn heißen;
stimmst du dem Vater bei, ist morgen er dein Mann.

(Senta macht eine zuckende schmerzliche Bewegung; ihre Haltung bleibt aber ruhig. Daland zeigt einen Schmuck hervor und zeigt ihn seiner Tochter.)

You stand rooted to the spot –
Senta, do I deserve such a greeting?

SENTA *(as Daland comes up to her, she grasps his hand)*
God give you greeting!

(drawing him closer to her)

Father, say,
who is this stranger?

DALAND *(smiling)*
Do you press me?
My child, will you bid this stranger welcome?   [32]
He is a seaman, like me, and asks our hospitality.
Long homeless, always on far, distant voyages,
in foreign lands he has gained great wealth.
Banished from his native land,
for a home he will pay handsomely:
speak, Senta, would it displease you
if this stranger stayed with us?

(Senta nods her approval; Daland turns to the Dutchman.)

Say, did I praise her too much?
You can see for yourself - does she please you?
Should I let my praises still overflow?
Confess, she is an ornament to her sex!

(The Dutchman makes a gesture of assent.)

If, my child, you show yourself well disposed to this man,
he also asks for the gracious gift of your heart; give him
your hand and you shall have him for a bridegroom; if you consent
to your father's suggestion, he will marry you tomorrow.

(Senta makes a convulsive movement of pain; she remains, however, composed. Daland produces some jewellery and shows it to his daughter.)

>Sieh dieses Band, sieh diese Spangen!
>Was er besitzt, macht dies gering.
>Muss, teures Kind, dich's nicht verlangen?
>Dein ist es, wechselst du den Ring.   [32]

(Senta, ohne ihn zu beachten, wendet ihren Blick nicht vom Holländer ab, sowie auch dieser, ohne auf Daland zu hören, nur in den Anblick des Mädchens versunken ist. Daland wird es gewahr; er betrachtet beide.)   [31]

>Doch keines spricht… Sollt' ich hier lästig sein?
>So ist's! Am besten lass ich sie allein.

(zu Senta)

>Mög'st du den edlen Mann gewinnen!
>Glaub' mir, solch Glück wird nimmer neu.

(zum Holländer)

>Bleibt hier allein! Ich geh' von hinnen.
>Glaubt mir, wie schön, so ist sie treu!   [32]

(Er geht langsam ab, indem er die beiden wohlgefällig und verwundert betrachtet. Senta und der Holländer allein. Lange Pause.)   [1]

HOLLÄNDER *(tief erschüttert)*
>Wie aus der Ferne längst vergang'ner Zeiten
>   spricht dieses Mädchens Bild zu mir:
>wie ich's geträumt seit bangen Ewigkeiten,
>   vor meinen Augen seh' ich's hier –
>Wohl hub auch ich voll Sehnsucht meine Blicke
>aus tiefer Nacht empor zu einem Weib:
>ein schlagend' Herz ließ, ach! mir Satans Tücke,
>dass eingedenk ich meiner Qualen bleib'.
>Die düst're Glut, die hier ich fühle brennen,
>sollt' ich Unseliger sie Liebe nennen?
>Ach nein! Die Sehnsucht ist es nach dem Heil:
>würd' es durch solchen Engel mir zuteil!

132

Look at this ring, look at these bracelets!
Of what he owns these are but a trifle.
Dear child, do you not long to have them?
All this is yours if you exchange rings. [32]

(Senta, disregarding him, does not take her eyes off the Dutchman who, likewise, without listening to Daland, is absorbed in contemplating her. Daland becomes aware of this; he looks at them both.) [31]

But neither speaks... Am I not wanted here?
I see! I'd better leave them alone.

(to Senta)

May you win this noble husband!
Believe me, such luck will not occur again.

(to the Dutchman)

Stay here alone! I will leave you.
Believe me, she is as true as she is fair! [32]

(He goes out slowly, watching them both with pleased surprise. Senta and the Dutchman are alone. Long pause.) [1]

DUTCHMAN *(deeply moved)*
This maiden's image speaks to me
    as from the distance of time long past:
as I had dreamt of it through eternities of dread,
    now I see it before my eyes. I lifted up my eyes,
from the depths of darkness,
full of longing for a wife;
ah! Satan's malice left me a heart to beat,
that I should remain mindful of my torment.
Can I, accursed as I am, call love
the dull glow that I feel burning here?
Ah, no! My longing is for release:
O, that it might come about through an angel like this!

133

SENTA

> Versank ich jetzt in wunderbares Träumen,
>> was ich erblicke, ist es Wahn?
> Weilt' ich bisher in trügerischen Räumen,
>> brach des Erwachens Tag heut' an?
> Er steht vor mir, mit leidenvollen Zügen,
>> es spricht sein unerhörter Gram zu mir:
> kann tiefen Mitleids Stimme mich belügen?
> Wie ich ihn oft geseh'n, so steht er hier.
> Die Schmerzen, die in meinem Busen brennen,
>> ach! dies' Verlangen, wie soll ich es nennen? –
> Wonach mit Sehnsucht es dich treibt – das Heil,
> würd' es, du Ärmster, dir durch mich zuteil! [5, 31]

HOLLÄNDER *(sich Senta etwas nähernd)*

> Wirst du des Vaters Wahl nicht schelten?
> Was er versprach, wie? – dürft' es gelten?
> Du könntest dich für ewig mir ergeben,
> und deine Hand dem Fremdling reichtest du?
> Soll finden ich, nach qualenvollem Leben
> in deiner Treu' die langersehnte Ruh'?

SENTA

> Wer du auch seist und welches das Verderben,
> dem grausam dich dein Schicksal konnte weih'n –
> was auch das Los, das ich mir sollt' erwerben:
> gehorsam stets werd' ich stets dem Vater sein!

HOLLÄNDER

> So unbedingt, wie? Könnte dich durchdringen
> für meine Leiden tiefstes Mitgefühl!

SENTA *(halb für sich)*

> O, welche Leiden! Könnt' ich Trost dir bringen!

HOLLÄNDER *(der es vernommen)*

> Welch' holder Klang im nächtlichen Gewühl! [5]
> Du bist ein Engel! Eines Engels Liebe
>> Verworf'ne selbst zu trösten weiß.

SENTA

Am I now deep in some wondrous dream?
    Is what I see a vision?
Have I been till now in realms of delusion?
    Has the day of awakening just dawned?
He stands before me, his features lined with sorrow,
his unspoken grief speaks to me:
can the voice of deep sympathy mislead me?
He is here as I have often seen him.
Ah, what can I call this longing,
these sorrows which burn in my bosom?
The release for which you yearn, poor man,
oh, that it might come about through me!   [5, 31]

DUTCHMAN *(drawing slightly nearer to Senta)*

    Are you not against your father's choice?
    Could what he promised – could it hold good?
Could you be mine for ever
and give your hand to me, a foreigner?
After a life of torment shall I find
in your true love my long-sought rest?

SENTA

Whoever you may be and whatever the doom
that cruel fate may decree for you –
whatever the lot that I bring upon myself,
I will always be obedient to my father.

DUTCHMAN

What, so unquestioningly? Could you be filled
with such deep compassion for my sorrows?

SENTA *(half aside)*

O, what sorrows! Could I bring you comfort!

DUTCHMAN *(who has heard this)*

How sweet a sound in my night of tumult!   [5]
You are an angel! An angel's love
    can comfort even lost souls.

Oh, wenn Erlösung mir zu hoffen bliebe,
   Allewiger, durch *diese* sei's!

SENTA *(für sich)*

   Ach, wenn Erlösung ihm zu hoffen bliebe,
     Allewiger, durch *mich* nur sei's!

HOLLÄNDER

   Oh, könntest das Geschick du ahnen,   [4]
   dem dann mit mir du angehörst,   [5]
   dich würd' es an das Opfer mahnen,
   das du mir bringst, wenn Treu' du schwörst.
   Es flöhe schaudernd deine Jugend
   dem Lose, dem du sie willst weih'n,
   nennst du des Weibes schönste Tugend,
   nennst ew'ge Treue du nicht dein!

SENTA

   Wohl kenn' ich Weibes heil'ge Pflichten,   [4]
   sei drum getrost, unsel'ger Mann!
   Lass über die das Schicksal richten,
   die seinem Spruche trotzen kann!
   In meines Herzens höchster Reine
   kenn' ich der Treue Hochgebot:
   wem ich sie weih', schenk' ich die *eine*,
     die Treue bis zum Tod.

HOLLÄNDER *(mit Erhebung)*

   Ein heil'ger Balsam meinen Wunden
   dem Schwur, dem hohen Wort entfließt.
   Hört es: mein Heil hab' ich gefunden,
   Mächte, die ihr zurück mich stießt.
   Du, Stern des Unheils, sollst erblassen.
   Licht meiner Hoffnung, leuchte neu!
   Ihr Engel, die mich einst verlassen,
   stärkt jetzt dies' Herz in seiner Treu'!

O, if I may still hope for redemption,
Eternal One, let it be through *her*!

SENTA *(aside)*

Ah, if he may still hope for redemption,
Eternal One, let it be through *me*!

DUTCHMAN

O, could you know the fate   [4]
that awaits you with me;   [5]
the sacrifice you bring me
when you swear to be true would daunt you.
Your youth would flee, shuddering,
from the lot you would bring upon yourself,
if you did not keep your vow
of woman's highest virtue, true constancy!

SENTA

Well I know woman's sacred duties;   [4]
therefore, take comfort, hapless man!
Let fate condemn one
who can defy its decree!
In the purity of my heart
I know the high demands of fidelity;
to him to whom I vow it, I pledge it *wholly*,
fidelity till death!

DUTCHMAN *(in exaltation)*

This vow, this solemn promise,
pours a holy balsam on my wounds.
Hear, ye powers! I have found my salvation,
which you have withheld from me!
Star of misfortune, you shall wane;
light of hope, shine anew!
Ye angels who once forsook me,
now strengthen her heart and keep her true!

SENTA

>Von mächt'gem Zauber überwunden
>reißt mich's zu seiner Rettung fort:
>hier habe Heimat er gefunden,
>hier ruh' sein Schiff in sich'rem Port!
>Was ist's, das mächtig in mir lebet? [33]
>Was schließt berauscht mein Busen ein?
>Allmächt'ger, was mich hoch erhebet,
>lass es die Kraft der Treue sein.

DALAND *(wieder eintretend)*

>Verzeiht! Mein Volk hält draußen sich nicht mehr; [34]
>nach jeder Rückkunft, wisset, gibt's ein Fest:
>verschönern möcht' ich's, komme deshalb her,
>ob mit Verlobung sich's vereinen lässt?

(zum Holländer)

>Ich denk', ihr habt nach Herzenswunsch gefreit?

(zu Senta)

>Senta, mein Kind, sag', bist auch du bereit?

SENTA *(mit feierlicher Entschlossenheit)*

>Hier meine Hand! Und ohne Reu'
>bis in den Tod gelob' ich Treu'!

HOLLÄNDER

>Sie reicht die Hand! Gesprochen sei
>Hohn, Hölle, dir durch ihre Treu'!

DALAND

>Euch soll dies Bündnis nicht gereu'n!
>Zum Fest! Heut' soll sich alles freu'n! [33]

SENTA

> Some mighty magic fires me
> and sends me forth to save him:
> here may he find a home,
> here may his ship rest in safe haven!
> What is this power I feel within me? [33]
> What enchantment is locked in my bosom?
> Almighty God, let this which elevates me
> be the strength of fidelity.

DALAND *(re-entering)*

> Forgive me! My people will stay outside no longer; [34]
> each time we return home, you know, there is a feast:
> I would enhance it; therefore, I come to ask
> if it can be combined with a betrothal?

(to the Dutchman)

> I think you've wooed her to your heart's content?

(to Senta)

> Senta, my child, do you too consent?

SENTA *(with solemn resolution)*

> Here is my hand! And without regret
> I plight my troth till death!

DUTCHMAN

> She gives her hand! Powers of hell,
> through her troth I defy you!

DALAND

> You shall not regret this union!
> To the feast! Today, let all rejoice! [33]

DRITTER AUFZUG

Seebucht mit felsigem Gestade: das Haus Dalands zur Seite im Vordergrunde.

Den Hintergrund nehmen, ziemlich nahe beieinander liegend, die beiden Schiffe, das des Norwegers und das des Holländers, ein.

Helle Nacht: das norwegische Schiff ist erleuchtet; die Matrosen desselben sind auf dem Verdeck; Jubel und Freude. Die Haltung des holländischen Schiffes bietet einen unheimlichen Kontrast: eine unnatürliche Finsternis ist über dasselbe ausgebreitet; es herrscht Totenstille auf ihm. [17, 14, 11]

Nr. 7 Szene und Chor

MATROSEN DES NORWEGERS *(trinkend)*

Steuermann, lass die Wacht! [11]

Steuermann, her zu uns!

Ho! He! Je! Ha! [14]

Hisst die Segel auf! Anker fest!

Steuermann, her!

Fürchten weder Wind noch bösen Strand,

wollen heute mal recht lustig sein!

Jeder hat sein Mädel auf dem Land,

herrlichen Tabak und guten Branntewein.

Hussassahe!

Klipp' und Sturm drauß' –

Jollohohe!

Lachen wir aus!

Hussassahe!

Segel ein! Anker fest! Klipp' und Sturm lachen wir aus!

Steuermann, lass die Wacht!

Steuermann, her zu uns!

Ho! He! Je! Ha!

ACT THREE

A bay with a rocky shore: Daland's house to one side in the fore-ground.

The background is occupied by the two ships, the Norwegian's and the Dutchman's, lying fairly close together.

The night is clear: the Norwegian ship is lit up; its sailors are on deck, making merry. The appearance of the Dutch ship presents an uncanny contrast; it is enveloped in unnatural gloom and deathly quiet. [17, 14, 11]

No. 7 Scene and chorus

NORWEGIAN SAILORS *(drinking)*

             Steersman, leave your watch! [11]
             Steersman, join us here!
             Ho! Hey! Hey! Ha! [14]
          Hoist sail! Drop anchor!
            Steersman, come here!
Fearing neither wind nor rocky shore,
today we'll be right merry!
Each one has a sweetheart ashore,
capital tobacco and good brandy wine.
             Hussassa hey!
For crag and storm out there…
               Yollo hohe!
         …we don't care a rap!
             Hussassa hey!
Furl sail! Anchor fast! At crag and storm we laugh!
          Steersman, leave your watch!
Steersman, join us here!
Ho! Hey! Hey! Ha!

Steuermann, her! Trink mit uns!
Ho! He! Je! Ha!
Klipp' und Sturm he!
Sind vorbei, he!
Hussahe! Hallohe!
Hussahe! Steuermann! Ho!
Her, komm und trink mit uns!

(Sie tanzen auf dem Verdeck, indem sie den Niederschlag jedes Taktes mit starkem Aufstampfen der Füße begleiten.

Die Mädchen kommen mit Körben voll Speisen und Getränken.) [17]

MÄDCHEN
Mein! Seht doch an! Sie tanzen gar!   [35]
Der Mädchen bedarf's da nicht, fürwahr!

(Sie gehen auf das holländische Schiff zu)

MATROSEN
He! Mädel! Halt! Wo geht ihr hin?

MÄDCHEN
Steht euch nach frischem Wein der Sinn?
Eu'r Nachbar dort soll auch was haben!
Ist Trank und Schmaus für euch allein?

STEUERMANN
Fürwahr! Tragt's hin den armen Knaben!
Vor Durst sie scheinen matt zu sein!

MATROSEN
Man hört sie nicht!

STEUERMANN
Ei, seht doch nur!
Kein Licht! Von der Mannschaft keine Spur!

MÄDCHEN *(im Begriff, an Bord des Holländers zu gehen)*
He! Seeleut'! He! Wollt Fackeln ihr?
Wo seid ihr doch? Man sieht nicht hier!

> Steersman, here! Drink with us!
> Ho! Hey! Hey! Ha!
> Crag and storm, hey!
> We've done with them!
> Hussa hey! Hallo hey!
> Hussa hey! Steersman! Ho!
> Here, come and drink with us!

(They dance on the deck, accompanying the downbeat of every bar with loud stamping of their feet.

The girls arrive with baskets full of food and drink.) [17]

GIRLS
> Oh, do look! They're dancing, indeed! [35]
> It's clear they don't need any girls.

(They go up to the Dutch ship.)

SAILORS
> Hey, girls! Stop! Where are you going?

GIRLS
> Do you fancy some refreshing wine?
> Your neighbour there should have some too!
> Is food and drink only for you?

STEERSMAN
> You're right! Take some to the poor lads!
> They seem to be faint with thirst!

SAILORS
> There's no sound from them.

STEERSMAN
> And just look! No lights!
> Not a trace of the crew!

GIRLS *(on the point of going aboard the Dutchman's ship)*
> Ho, sailors! Hey! Do you want some light?
> Where are you then? We can't see you!

143

MATROSEN *(lachend)*
Hahaha!
Weckt sie nicht auf! Sie schlafen noch.

MÄDCHEN *(in das Schiff hineinrufend)*
He! Seeleut! He! Antwortet doch!

(Große Stille.)   [36]

STEUERMANN und MATROSEN
Haha!

(spöttisch, mit affektierter Traurigkeit)

Wahrhaftig! Sie sind tot:
sie haben Speis' und Trank nicht not!

MÄDCHEN *(wie oben)*
Wie, Seeleute? Liegt ihr so faul schon im Nest?
Ist heute für euch denn nicht auch ein Fest?

MATROSEN *(wie vorher)*
Sie liegen fest auf ihrem Platz,
wie Drachen hüten sie den Schatz.

MÄDCHEN
He, Seeleute! Wollt ihr nicht frischen Wein?
Ihr müsset wahrlich doch durstig auch sein!

MATROSEN
Sie trinken nicht, sie singen nicht;
in ihrem Schiffe brennt kein Licht.

MÄDCHEN
Sagt! Habt ihr denn nicht auch ein Schätzchen am Land?
Wollt ihr nicht mit tanzen auf freundlichem Strand?

MATROSEN
Sie sind schon alt und bleich statt rot!
und ihre Liebsten, die sind tot!

SAILORS *(laughing)*
    Ha ha ha!
    Don't wake them! They're still asleep.

GIRLS *(shouting to the ship)*
    Hey, sailors! Hey! Answer us!

(Complete silence.)   [36]

STEERSMAN and SAILORS
    Ha ha!

(mockingly, with affected sorrow)

    They're dead, for sure;
    they don't need food and drink!

GIRLS
    Hey, sailors! Are you already snugly tucked up in bed?
    Isn't today a feast for you too?

SAILORS
    They stay lying where they are
    like dragons guarding their gold.

GIRLS
    Hey, sailors! Don't you want some refreshing wine?
    You must surely be thirsty!

SAILORS
    They don't drink, they don't sing;
    there's no light aboard their ship.

GIRLS
    Say, haven't you any sweethearts on land?
    Won't you join the dancing on this friendly shore?

SAILORS
    They're old and grey, not ruddy!
    And their sweethearts are all dead!

MÄDCHEN *(heftig rufend)*
He! Seeleut'! Seeleut'! Wacht doch auf!
Wir bringen euch Speise und Trank zu Hauf!

MATROSEN *(verstärkend)*
He! Seeleut'! Seeleut'! Wacht doch auf!

(Langes Stillschweigen.)   [36]

MÄDCHEN *(betroffen und furchtsam)*
Wahrhaftig, ja! Sie scheinen tot! .
Sie haben Speis' und Trank nicht not.

MATROSEN *(lustig)*
Vom fliegenden Holländer wisst ihr ja!
Sein Schiff, wie es leibt, wie es lebt, seht ihr da!

MÄDCHEN
So weckt die Mannschaft ja nicht auf:
Gespenster sind's, wir schwören drauf!

MATROSEN *(mit steigender Ausgelassenheit)*
Wie viel hundert Jahre schon seid ihr zur See?
Euch tut ja der Sturm und die Klippe nicht weh!

MÄDCHEN
Sie trinken nicht! Sie singen nicht!
In ihrem Schiffe brennt kein Licht.

MATROSEN
Habt ihr keine Brief', keine Aufträg' für's Land?
Uns'ren Urgroßvätern wir bringen's zur Hand!

MÄDCHEN
Sie sind schon alt und bleich statt rot!
Und ihre Liebsten, ach, sind tot!

MATROSEN *(lärmend)*
Hei, Seeleute! Spannt eure Segel doch auf
und zeigt uns des fliegenden Holländers Lauf!

GIRLS *(calling loudly)*
    Hey, sailors! Sailors! Wake up, there!
    We bring you lots of food and drink!

SAILORS *(reinforcing them)*
    Hey, sailors! Sailors! Wake up, there!

(Long silence.)   [36]

GIRLS *(disconcerted and fearful)*
    Indeed, they do seem dead.
    They don't need food and drink.

SAILORS *(cheerfully)*
    You've heard of the Flying Dutchman!
    That's the very image of his ship you see!

GIRLS
    Then don't waken the crew:
    they're all ghosts, we're certain of it!

SAILORS *(with growing boisterousness)*
    How many centuries have you been at sea?
    Tempests and rocks don't harm you!

GIRLS
    They don't drink, they don't sing!
    There's no light aboard their ship.

SAILORS
    Have you no letters, no messages for land?
    We'll hand them to our great-grandfathers!

GIRLS
    They're old and grey, not ruddy!
    And their sweethearts are all dead!

SAILORS *(noisily)*
    Hey, sailors! Spread your sails
    and show us how the Dutchman can fly!

MÄDCHEN *(sich mit ihren Körben furchtsam vom holländischen Schiffe entfernend)*
Sie hören nicht! Uns graust es hier!
Sie wollen nichts – was rufen wir?

MATROSEN
Ihr Mädel, lasst die Toten ruh'n!
Lasst's uns Lebend'gen gütlich tun!

MÄDCHEN *(den Matrosen ihre Körbe über Bord reichend)*
So nehmt! Der Nachbar hat's verschmäht!

STEUERMANN
Wie? Kommt ihr denn nicht selbst an Bord?

MATROSEN
Wie? Kommt ihr denn nicht selbst an Bord?

MÄDCHEN
Ei, jetzt noch nicht! Es ist ja nicht spät!
Wir kommen bald! Jetzt trinkt nur fort,
und, wenn ihr wollt, so tanzt dazu,
nur gönnt dem müden Nachbar Ruh'.

(Sie gehen ab.)

MATROSEN *(die Körbe leerend)*
Juchhe! Juchhe! Da gibt's die Fülle!
Lieb' Nachbar, habe Dank!

STEUERMANN
Zum Rand sein Glas ein jeder fülle!
Lieb' Nachbar liefert uns den Trank.

MATROSEN *(jubelnd)*
Hallohohoho!
Lieb Nachbarn, habt ihr Stimm' und Sprach',
so wachet auf und macht's uns nach! Hussa! [37]

148

GIRLS *(frightened, retreating with their baskets from the Dutch ship)*
   They don't hear! And we're afraid!
   They want nothing – so why do we shout?

SAILORS
   You girls, leave the dead in peace!
   Let us, the living, enjoy ourselves!

GIRLS *(handing their baskets to the sailors on board)*
   Then take it! Your neighbours reject it.

STEERSMAN
   What? Aren't you yourselves coming aboard?

SAILORS
   What? Aren't you yourselves coming aboard?

GIRLS
   No, not just yet! It isn't late!
   We'll come soon! Now drink away,
   and if you like, dance too;
   but don't grudge your weary neighbours rest.

(Exeunt.)

SAILORS *(emptying the baskets)*
   Hurrah! Hurrah! There's plenty here!
   Thank you, dear neighbours!

STEERSMAN
   Everyone fill his glass to the brim!
   Our dear neighbours have supplied us with drink.

SAILORS *(jubilantly)*
   Hallohohoho!
   Dear neighbours, if you have tongues at all,
   wake up and join us! Hussa!   [37]

149

(Sie trinken aus und stampfen die Becher heftig auf.)

(Von hier an beginnt es sich auf dem holländischen Schiff zu regen.)

Steuermann, lass die Wacht! [11]
Steuermann! her zu uns!
Ho! He! Je! Ha! [14]
Hisst die Segel auf! Anker fest!
Steuermann her!
Wachten manche Nacht im Sturm und Graus,
tranken oft des Meer's gesalz'nes Nass:
heute wachen wir bei Saus und Schmaus,
besseres Getränk gibt Mädel uns vom Fass.
Hussassahe!
Klipp' und Sturm drauß' –
Jollohohe!
Hussassahe!
Segel ein! Anker fest! Klipp' und Sturm lachen wir aus!
Steuermann, lass die Wacht!
Steuermann, her zu uns!
Ho! He! Je! Ha!
Steuermann, her! Trink' mit uns! [17]
Ho! He! Je! Ha!
Klipp' und Sturm, he!
Sind vorbei, he!
Hussahe! Hallohe!
Hussahe! Steuermann! Ho!
Her, komm und trink mit uns! [17]

(Das Meer, das sonst überall ruhig bleibt, hat sich im Umkreise des holländischen Schiffes zu heben begonnen; eine düstere, bläuliche Flamme lodert in diesem als Wachtfeuer auf. Sturmwind erhebt sich in dessen Tauen. Die Mannschaft, von der man zuvor nichts sah, belebt sich)

DIE MANNSCHAFT DES HOLLÄNDERS
Johohoe! Johohoe! Hoe! Hoe! [1, 14]
Hui–ßa! [15]
Nach dem Land treibt der Sturm. [2]

(They drink up and set down the cups noisily.)

(From here on there are stirrings of life on the Dutch ship.)

Steersman, leave your watch!	[11]
Steersman, join us here!	
Ho! Hey! Hey! Ha!	[14]

Hoist sail! Drop anchor!
Steersman, come here!
Many a night we've watched in howling storms,
often drunk the sea's briny waters;
today, making merry, we watch
our girls give us a better drink from the barrel.
Hussassa hey!
For crag and storm out there…
Yolloho hey!
Hussassa hey!
Furl sail! Anchor fast! At crag and storm we laugh!
Steersman, leave your watch!
Steersman, join us here!
Ho! Hey! Hey! Ha!
Steersman, here drink with us! [17]
Ho! Hey! Hey! Ha!
Crag and storm, hey!
we've done with them!
Hussa hey! Hallo hey!
Hussa hey! Steersman! Ho!
Here, come and drink with us! [17]

(The sea, which everywhere else remains calm, has begun to rise in the neighbourhood of the Dutch ship; a dull blue flame flares up like a watchfire. A storm wind whistles through the rigging. The crew, hitherto invisible, bestir themselves.)

THE DUTCHMAN'S CREW

Yohohoe! Yohohoe! Hoe! Hoe!	[1, 14]
Hui–ssa!	[15]
Onto shore drives the storm.	[2]

Hui–ßa!
Segel ein! Anker los!
Hui–ßa!
In die Bucht laufet ein! [30]
Schwarzer Hauptmann, geh' ans Land,
sieben Jahre sind vorbei!
Frei' um blonden Mädchens Hand!
Blondes Mädchen, sei ihm treu'!
Lustig heut', hui!
Bräutigam! Hui!
Sturmwind heult Brautmusik – Ozean tanzt dazu!
Hui! – Horch, er pfeift! – [15]
– Kapitän, bist wieder da? –
Hui! – Segel auf! –
Deine Braut, sag', wo sie blieb? –
– Hui! – Auf, in See! –
Kapitän! Kapitän! Hast kein Glück in der Lieb'!
Hahaha!
Sause, Sturmwind, heute zu! [1, 2]
Uns'ren Segeln lässt du Ruh'!
Satan hat sie uns gefeit,
reißen nicht in Ewigkeit!
Hohoe! nicht in Ewigkeit!

(Während des Gesanges der Holländer wird ihr Schiff von den Wogen auf und ab getragen; furchtbarer Sturmwind heult und pfeift durch die nackten Taue. Die Luft und das Meer bleiben übrigens, außer in der nächsten Umgebung des holländischen Schiffes, ruhig wie zuvor.)

DIE NORWEGISCHEN MATROSEN *(die erst mit Verwun-derung, dann mit Entsetzen zugehört und zugesehen haben)*
Welcher Sang! Ist es Spuk? – Wie mich's graut!
Stimmet an – unser Lied! – Singet laut! –
Steuermann, lass die Wacht! [11]
Steuermann, her zu uns!
Ho! He! Je! Ha!

        Hui–ssa!
Furl sail! Down with the anchor!
Hui–ssa!
Hurry in to the bay!   [30]
Gloomy captain, go ashore,
seven years are up!
Seek a blonde maiden's hand!
Blonde maiden, be true to him!
        Be joyful today, whee!
        Bridegroom! Whee!
The storm wind howls bridal music – the ocean dances to it!
        Whee! Hark, it whistles! –   [15]
        Captain, are you back again? –
        Whee! Set sail! –
        Your bride, oh where is she? –
        Whee! Off to sea! –
Captain! Captain! You're not lucky in love!
        Ha ha ha!
        Storm wind, blow and howl,   [1, 2]
        you can't perturb our sails!
        Satan has given them his blessing,
        in all eternity they'll not burst.
Hohoe! Not in all eternity!

(During the Dutchman's crew's song their ship is tossed up and down by the waves; a terrible storm wind howls and whistles through the bare rigging. The air and sea elsewhere, except in the immediate neighbourhood of the Dutch ship, remains calm, as before.)

NORWEGIAN SAILORS *(who have watched and listened first with astonishment, then with terror)*
What a song! Are they ghosts? – I'm filled with fear!
Sing our song! Sing loudly!
        Steersman, leave your watch!   [11]
        Steersman, join us here!
        Ho! Hey! Hey! Ha!

(Der Gesang der Mannschaft des Holländers wird in einzelnen Strophen immer stärker wiederholt; die Norweger suchen ihn mit ihrem Liede zu übertäuben; nach vergeblichen Versuchen bringt sie das Tosen des Meeres, das Sausen, Heulen und Pfeifen des unnatürlichen Sturmes sowie der immer wilder werdende Gesang der Holländer zum Schweigen. Sie ziehen sich zurück, schlagen das Kreuz und verlassen das Verdeck; die Holländer, als sie dies sehen, erheben ein gellendes Hohngelächter. Sodann herrscht mit einem Male auf ihrem Schiffe wieder die erste Totenstille; Luft und Meer werden in einem Augenblick wieder ruhig, wie zuvor.) [36]

Nr. 8 Finale

(Senta kommt bewegten Schrittes aus dem Hause; ihr folgt Erik in höchster Aufregung.)

ERIK

Was musst' ich hören? Gott, was musst' ich sehen?
Ist's Täuschung? Wahrheit? Ist es Tat?

SENTA *(sich mit peinlichem Gefühle abwendend)*

Oh, frage nicht! Antwort darf ich nicht geben. [38]

ERIK

Gerechter Gott! Kein Zweifel! Es ist wahr!
Welch' unheilvolle Macht riss dich dahin?
Welche Gewalt verführte dich so schnell, [39]
grausam zu brechen dieses treuste Herz!
Dein Vater – ha! den Bräut'gam bracht' er mit...
Wohl kenn' ich ihn... mir ahnte, was geschieht!
Doch du... ist's möglich! – reichest deine Hand
dem Mann, der deine Schwelle kaum betrat!

SENTA

Nicht weiter! Schweig'! Ich muss, ich muss!

154

(The song of the Dutchman's crew is repeated, getting louder with each stanza; the Norwegians try to drown the song of the Dutchman's crew with their own song. After vain efforts, the raging of the sea, the roaring, howling and whistling of the unnatural storm, together with the ever-wilder song of the Dutchman's crew silence them. They fall back, make the sign of the cross and quit the deck; the Dutch crew, seeing them, burst into shrill, mocking laughter. After this, the former deathlike silence suddenly falls on their ship again; in a moment, air and sea become calm, as before.) [36]

No. 8 Finale

(Senta comes hurrying out of the house; Erik follows her in great agitation.)

ERIK

Must I hear this? God, must I see this?
Is this delusion or the truth? Can it be?

SENTA *(turning away, painfully moved)*

O, do not ask! I dare not answer you. [38]

ERIK

Righteous heaven! Beyond doubt, it is true!
What unholy power led you astray?
What power so quickly induced you [39]
cruelly to break my faithful heart?
Your father – ah! he brought the bridegroom with him...
I know him well... I suspected what would happen!
But you... is it possible! – you gave your hand
to a man who has barely crossed your threshold!

SENTA

No more! Hush! I must, I must!

155

ERIK

O des Gehorsams, blind wie deine Tat! [39]
Den Wink des Vaters nanntest du willkommen,
mit einem Stoß vernichtest du mein Herz!

SENTA *(mit sich kämpfend)*

Nicht mehr! Nicht mehr! Ich darf dich nicht mehr seh'n,
nicht an dich denken: hohe Pflicht gebeut's.

ERIK

Welch' hohe Pflicht? Ist's höh're nicht, zu halten,
was du mir einst gelobtest, ewige Treue?

SENTA *(heftig erschrocken)*

Wie? Ew'ge Treue hätt' ich dir gelobt?

ERIK *(mit Schmerz)*

Senta, o Senta, leugnest du?
Willst jenes Tags du nicht mehr dich entsinnen, [40]
als du zu dir mich riefest in das Tal?
Als, dir des Hochlands Blume zu gewinnen,
mutvoll ich trug Beschwerden ohne Zahl?
Gedenkst du, wie auf steilem Felsenriffe
vom Ufer wir den Vater scheiden sah'n?
Er zog dahin auf weiß beschwingtem Schiffe,
und meinem Schutz vertraute er dich an.
Als sich dein Arm um meinen Nacken schlang,
gestandest du mir Liebe nicht aufs neu'?
Was bei der Hände Druck mich hehr durchdrang,
sag', war's nicht Versich'rung deiner Treu'?

(Der Holländer hat den Auftritt belauscht; in furchtbarer Aufregung bricht er jetzt hervor.)

HOLLÄNDER

Verloren! Ach, verloren! Ewig verlor'nes Heil!

ERIK *(entsetzt zurücktretend)*

Was seh' ich? Gott!

ERIK

O, this obedience! Blind as what you have done!   [39]
You welcomed your father's suggestion,
with a single blow you break my heart!

SENTA *(struggling with herself)*

No more! No more! I must not see you again,
nor think of you: sacred duty commands it.

ERIK

What sacred duty? Is it not more sacred
to keep the eternal faith you once pledged to me?

SENTA *(frightened)*

What? I pledged eternal faith to you?

ERIK *(sorrowfully)*

Senta, O Senta, can you deny it?
Do you no longer remember that day   [40]
when you called me to you in the valley?
When, to cull mountain flowers for you,
I fearlessly took countless pains?
Do you recall how on the steep rocky ridge
we watched your father depart from the shore?
He sailed away on his white-winged ship
and entrusted you to my care.
When you put your arm around my neck
did you not confess your love anew?
What thrilled me in the clasp of our hand,
say, was that not the affirmation of your troth?

(The Dutchman, unnoticed, has heard all this: in terrible agitation he now bursts in.)

DUTCHMAN

Lost! Ah, lost! Salvation is lost for ever!

ERIK *(recoiling in terror)*

What do I see? Heavens!

157

HOLLÄNDER
Senta, leb' wohl!

SENTA *(sich ihm in den Weg werfend)*
Halt' ein, Unsel'ger!

ERIK *(zu Senta)*
Was beginnst du?

HOLLÄNDER
In See! In See – für ew'ge Zeiten!

(zu Senta)

Um deine Treue ist's getan,
um deine Treue – um mein Heil!
Leb' wohl, ich will dich nicht verderben!

ERIK
Entsetzlich! Dieser Blick… !

SENTA
Halt' ein!
Von dannen sollst du nimmer flieh'n!

HOLLÄNDER *(gibt seiner Mannschaft ein gellendes Zeichen auf einer Schiffspfeife)*
Segel auf! Anker los!   [15, 2, 3]
Sagt Lebewohl für Ewigkeit dem Lande!

SENTA
Ha! Zweifelst du an meiner Treue?   [38]
Unsel'ger, was verblendet dich?
Halt' ein! Das Bündnis nicht bereue!
Was ich gelobte, halte ich!

HOLLÄNDER
Fort auf das Meer triebt's mich auf's neue!
Ich zweifl' an dir, ich zweifl' an Gott!
Dahin! Dahin ist alle Treue!
Was du gelobtest, war dir Spott!

158

DUTCHMAN
Senta, farewell!

SENTA *(throwing herself in his path)*
Stop, unhappy man!

ERIK *(to Senta)*
What are you going to do?

DUTCHMAN
To sea! To sea – for all eternity!

(to Senta)

There's an end to your vow,
to your vow – and my salvation!
Farewell, you shall not perish with me!

ERIK
O, horror! That look!…

SENTA
Stop!
You shall never flee from here!

DUTCHMAN *(giving his crew a shrill signal on his whistle)*
Set sail! Up anchor!   [15, 2, 3]
Bid farewell to the land for ever!

SENTA
Ah, you doubt my faith?   [38]
Unhappy man, what has misled you?
O, stay! Do not repent our bond!
I will hold to what I promised!

DUTCHMAN
I am driven forth to sea once more!
I cannot depend on you, I cannot depend on God!
All trust is lost, lost!
What you pledged was but in jest!

ERIK

> Was hör' ich! Gott, was muss ich sehen?
> Muss ich dem Ohr, dem Auge trau'n?
> Senta! Willst du zugrunde gehen?
> Zu mir! Du bist in Satans Klau'n!

HOLLÄNDER

Erfahre das Geschick, vor dem ich dich bewahre!
Verdammt bin ich zum grässlichsten der Lose:
zehnfacher Tod wär' mir erwünschte Lust!
Vom Fluch ein Weib allein kann mich erlösen,
ein Weib, das Treu' bis in den Tod mir hält…
Wohl hast du Treue mir gelobt, doch vor
dem Ewigen noch nicht: dies rettet dich!
Denn wiss', Unsel'ge, welches das Geschick,
das jene trifft, die mir die Treue brechen:
ew'ge Verdammnis ist ihr Los!
Zahllose Opfer fielen diesem Spruch
durch mich! Du aber sollst gerettet sein.
Leb' wohl! Fahr' hin, mein Heil, in Ewigkeit!

ERIK *(in furchtbarer Angst nach dem Hause und dem Schiffe zu rufend)*

Zu Hilfe! Rettet! Rettet sie!

SENTA *(in höchster Aufregung)*

Wohl kenn' ich dich! Wohl kenn' ich dein Geschick!
Ich kannte dich, als ich zuerst dich sah!
Das Ende deiner Qual ist da! – Ich bin's,
durch deren Treu' dein Heil du finden sollst!

(Auf Eriks Hilferufe sind Daland, Mary und die Mädchen aus dem Hause, die Matrosen von dem Schiffe herbeigeeilt.)

ERIK

Helft ihr! Sie ist verloren!

DALAND, MARY und CHOR

> Was erblick' ich!

ERIK

What do I hear? O God, what must I see?
Must I believe my eyes and ears?
Senta! Are you bent on destruction?
Come to me! You are in Satan's clutches!

DUTCHMAN

Learn the fate from which I save you!
I am doomed to the most hideous of lots:
rather would I welcome death ten times over!
From the curse, a woman alone can free me,
a woman who would be true to me till death...
You plighted your troth to me, but not
before Almighty God: this saves you!
For know, unhappy maid, what is the fate
awaiting those who break their vow to me:
    eternal damnation is their lot!
Countless victims have suffered this sentence
through me; but you shall escape.
Farewell! All hope be lost for ever!

ERIK *(in fearful terror, calling to the house and the ship)*
Help! Save her, save her!

SENTA *(in the utmost excitement)*
Well I know you! Well I know your fate!
I knew you when first I saw you!
The end of your torment is at hand! I am she
through whose constancy you shall find salvation!

*(At Erik's cries for help, Daland, Mary and the girls have hurried
from the house, and the sailors from the ship.)*

ERIK

Help her! She is lost!

DALAND, MARY and CHORUS
                    What do I see?

DALAND
Gott!

HOLLÄNDER *(zu Senta)*
Du kennst mich nicht, du ahnst nicht, wer ich bin!

(Er deutet auf sein Schiff, dessen rote Segel aufgespannt sind und dessen Mannschaft in gespenstischer Regsamkeit die Abfahrt vorbereitet.)

Befrag die Meere aller Zonen, befrag
den Seemann, der den Ozean durchstrich,
er kennt dies Schiff, das Schrecken aller Frommen:
den *fliegenden Holländer* nennt man mich!

DIE MANNSCHAFT DES HOLLÄNDERS
Johohe! Johohoe! Hoe! Huißa!   [1, 14]

(Mit Blitzesschnelle langt er am Bord seines Schiffes an, das augenblicklich unter dem Seerufe der Mannschaft abfährt. Alles steht entsetzt. Senta sucht sich mit Gewalt von Daland und Erik, die sie halten, loszuwinden.)

DALAND, ERIK, MARY und CHOR
Senta! Senta! Was willst du tun?

(Senta hat sich mit wütender Macht losgerissen und erreicht ein vorstehendes Felsenriff: von da aus ruft sie mit aller Gewalt dem absegelnden Holländer nach.)

SENTA
Preis' deinen Engel und sein Gebot!
Hier steh' ich treu dir bis zum Tod!

(Sie stürzt sich in das Meer; in demselben Augenblicke versinkt das Schiff des Holländers und verschwindet schnell in Trümmern. In weiter Ferne entsteigen dem Wasser der Holländer und Senta, beide in verklärter Gestalt; er hält sie umschlungen.)   [5, 12, 1]

DALAND
  O God!

DUTCHMAN *(to Senta)*
  You know me not, nor suspect who I am!

(He points to his ship, whose red sails are spread and whose crew, in ghostly activity, are preparing for departure.)

  But ask the seas throughout the world,
  ask the sailor who has crossed the ocean;
  he knows this ship, the dread of the godly:
  I am called the *Flying Dutchman*.

THE DUTCHMAN'S CREW
  Yohohe! Yohohoe! Hoe! Huissa!   [1, 14]

(With lightning speed he boards his ship, which immediately puts to sea to the shouts of her crew. All stand aghast. Senta struggles to free herself from Daland and Erik, who hold her back.)

DALAND, ERIK, MARY and CHORUS
  Senta! Senta! What would you do?

(Senta, with a furious effort, has torn herself free and has reached a projecting rocky ridge; from there she calls after the departing Dutchman with all her might.)

SENTA
  Praise your angel and his words!
  Here I am, true to you till death!

(She flings herself into the sea; at that same moment the Dutchman's ship sinks and quickly disappears as a wreck. In the far distance the Dutchman and Senta, he embracing her, rise from the water, both transfigured.)   [5, 12, 1]

Select Discography

For more detailed information of historical and off-the-air recordings of an earlier era, see Barry Millington, '*Der fliegende Holländer* (1843)', *The Metropolitan Opera Guide to Recorded Opera*, ed. Paul Gruber (London and New York: Thames and Hudson, 1993), pp. 670–76.

Except where indicated, all recordings are of the 1860 revised score, but played in one act.

YEAR	CAST	CONDUCTOR / ORCHESTRA	LABEL
	HOLLÄNDER		
	SENTA		
	DALAND		
	ERIK		
	MARY		
	STEUERMANN		
1936*	Fred Destal	Fritz Busch	Pearl
	Marjorie Lawrence	Teatro Colón,	(live)
	Alexander Kipnis	Buenos Aires	1860 version
	René Maison		played in
	Irra Petina		three acts
	Hans Fleischer		
1944*	Hans Hotter	Clemens Krauss	Preiser
	Viorica Ursuleac	Bayerische Staatsoper	1860 version
	Georg Hann		played in
	Karl Ostertag		three acts
	Luise Willer		
	Franz Klarwein		

1950*	Hans Hotter Astrid Varnay Sven Nilsson Set Svanholm Herta Glaz Thomas Hayward	Fritz Reiner Metropolitan Opera	Naxos (live) 1860 version played in three acts
1955	Hermann Uhde Astrid Varnay Ludwig Weber Wolfgang Windgassen Elisabeth Schärtel Josef Traxel	Hans Knappertsbusch Bayreuth Festival	Orfeo (live)
1955	Hermann Uhde Astrid Varnay Ludwig Weber Rudolf Lustig Elisabeth Schärtel Josef Traxel	Joseph Keilberth Bayreuth Festival	Testament (Decca) (live)
1959*	George London Leonie Rysanek Josef Greindl Fritz Uhl Res Fischer Georg Paskuda	Wolfgang Sawallisch Bayreuth Festival	Myto (live) Wieland Wagner's amended 1860 version played in three acts
1960	Dietrich Fischer-Dieskau Marianne Schech Gottlob Frick Rudolf Schock Sieglinde Wagner Fritz Wunderlich	Franz Konwitschny Berlin Staatsoper	Berlin Classics (EMI)
1960	George London Leonie Rysanek Giorgio Tozzi Karl Liebl Belén Amparan William Olvis	Thomas Schippers Metropolitan Opera	Walhall (live)

1961	George London Leonie Rysanek Giorgio Tozzi Karl Liebl Rosalind Elias Richard Lewis	Antal Doráti Royal Opera House, Covent Garden	Decca
1961	Franz Crass Anja Silja Josef Greindl Fritz Uhl Res Fischer Georg Paskuda	Wolfgang Sawallisch Bayreuth Festival	Philips (live) Wieland Wagner's amended 1860 version played in three acts
1968	Theo Adam Anja Silja Martti Talvela Ernst Kozub Annelies Burmeister Gerhard Unger	Otto Klemperer New Philharmonia	EMI Classics 1843 version
1968	Theo Adam Anja Silja Martti Talvela James King Annelies Burmeister Kenneth MacDonald	Otto Klemperer New Philharmonia	Testament (live) 1843 version
1971	Thomas Stewart Gwyneth Jones Karl Ridderbusch Hermin Esser Sieglinde Wagner Harald Ek	Karl Böhm Bayreuth Festival	DG (live)
1976	Norman Bailey Janis Martin Martti Talvela René Kollo Isola Jones Werner Krenn	Georg Solti Chicago Symphony	Decca

1983	José van Dam Dunja Vejzović Kurt Moll Peter Hofmann Kaja Borris Thomas Moser	Herbert von Karajan Berlin Philharmonic	EMI Classics
1985	Simon Estes Lisbeth Baslev Matti Salminen Robert Schunk Anny Schlemm Graham Clark	Woldemar Nelsson Bayreuth Festival	Philips (live) 1843 version played in one act
1991	Bernd Weikl Cheryl Studer Hans Sotin Plácido Domingo Uta Priew Peter Seiffert	Giuseppe Sinopoli Berlin Staatskapelle	DG
1991	Robert Hale Hildegard Behrens Kurt Rydl Josef Protschka Iris Vermillion Uwe Heilmann	Christoph von Dohnányi Vienna Philharmonic	Decca
1992	Alfred Muff Ingrid Haubold Erich Knodt Peter Seiffert Marga Schiml Jörg Hering	Pinchas Steinberg Austrian Radio Symphony (ORS)	Naxos
2001	Falk Struckmann Jane Eaglen Robert Holl Peter Seiffert Felicity Palmer Rolando Villazón	Daniel Barenboim Berlin Philharmonic	Teldec

2004	John Tomlinson Nina Stemme Eric Halfvarson Kim Begley Patricia Bardon Peter Wedd	David Parry London Philharmonic	Chandos (in English)
2004	Terje Stensvold Astrid Weber Franz-Josef Selig Jörg Dürmüller Simone Schröder Kobie van Rensburg	Bruno Weil Cappella Coloniensis	DHM (live) 1841 version played in one act with original Scottish names and on period instruments
2011	Albert Dohmen Ricarda Merbeth Matti Salminen Robert Dean Smith Silvia Hablowetz Steve Davislim	Marek Janowski Berlin Radio Symphony	PentaTone (live)

*mono

Der fliegende Holländer on DVD: a Selection

For more detailed information, including non-commercial and television films, up to 2004, see Ken Wlaschin, *Encyclopedia of Opera on Screen* (New Haven and London: Yale University Press, 2004), pp. 252–253.

YEAR	CAST	CONDUCTOR	DIRECTOR / COMPANY / LABEL
	HOLLÄNDER		
	SENTA		
	DALAND		
	ERIK		
	MARY		
	STEUERMANN		
1964*	Rainer Lüdeke (voice)/	Rolf Reuter	Joachim Herz
	Fred Dueren (acting)		Feature film
	Gerda Hannemann (voice)/		Dreamlife
	Anna Prucnal (acting)		(VHS / laser disc)
	Hans Krämer (voice)/		
	Gerd Ehlers (acting)		
	Rolf Apreck (voice)/		
	Herbert Graedke (acting)		
	Katrin Wölzl (voice)/		
	Mathilde Danegger (acting)		
	Friedrich Hölze (voice)/		
	Hans-Peter Reineck (acting)		

1975	Donald McIntyre	Wolfgang	Václav Kaslik
	Catarina Ligendza	Sawallisch	Studio film of
	Bengt Rundgren		Bavarian State Opera
	Hermann Winkler		production
	Ruth Hesse		DG
	Harald Ek		
1984	Simon Estes	Woldemar	Harry Kupfer
	Lisbeth Baslev	Nelsson	Bayreuth Festival
	Matti Salminen		Philips
	Robert Schunk		
	Anny Schlemm		
	Graham Clark		
1989	Franz Grundheber	Leif Segerstam	Ikka Bäckmann
	Hildegard Behrens		Savonlinna Opera
	Matti Salminen		Festival
	Raimo Sirkiä		Teldec
	Anita Välkki		
	Jorma Silvasti		
1991	Robert Hale	Wolfgang	Henning von Gierke
	Julia Varady	Sawallisch	Bayerische Staatsoper
	Jaako Rhyänen		EMI
	Peter Seiffert		
	Anny Schlemm		
	Ulrich Ress		
2010	Juha Uusitalo	Hartmut	Martin Kušej
	Catherine Naglestad	Haenchen	De Nederlandse Opera
	Robert Lloyd		Opus Arte
	Marco Jentzsch		
	Marina Prudenskaja		
	Oliver Ringelhahn		

*black and white

Select Bibliography

Borchmeyer, Dieter, *Drama and the World of Richard Wagner*, trans. Daphne Ellis (Princeton and Oxford: Princeton University Press, 2003)

Carnegy, Patrick, *Wagner and the Art of the Theatre* (New Haven and London: Yale University Press, 2006)

Deathridge, John, *Wagner beyond Good and Evil* (Berkeley and Los Angeles: University of California Press, 2008)

Dreyfus, Laurence, *Wagner and the Erotic Impulse* (Cambridge, Massachusetts and London: Harvard University Press, 2010)

Emslie, Barry, *Richard Wagner and the Centrality of Love* (New York: Boydell & Brewer, 2010)

Grey, Thomas (ed.), *Richard Wagner: Der fliegende Holländer* (Cambridge: Cambridge University Press, 2000)

Grey, Thomas (ed.), *The Cambridge Companion to Wagner* (Cambridge: Cambridge University Press, 2008)

Gutman, Robert W., *Richard Wagner: The Man, His Mind, and His Music* (New York: Harcourt, Brace & World, 1968)

Köhler, Joachim, *Richard Wagner: The Last of the Titans* (New Haven, CT and London: Yale University Press, 2004)

Millington, Barry (ed.), *The Wagner Compendium* (London: Thames and Hudson, 1992)

Millington, Barry and Spencer, Stewart (eds.), *Wagner in Performance* (New Haven and London: Yale University Press, 1992)

Newman, Ernest, *The Life of Richard Wagner*, 4 vols. (London: Cassell, 1933–47; New York: Knopf, 1946)

Spencer, Stewart, *Wagner Remembered* (London: Faber and Faber, 2000)

Spotts, Frederic, *Bayreuth: A History of the Bayreuth Festival* (New Haven and London: Yale University Press, 1994)

Tanner, Michael, *The Faber Pocket Guide to Wagner* (London: Faber and Faber, 2010)

Treadwell, James, *Interpreting Wagner* (New Haven and London: Yale University Press, 2003)

Vazsonyi, Nicholas (ed.), *The Cambridge Wagner Encyclopedia* (Cambridge: Cambridge University Press, to be published in 2013)

Wagner, Cosima, *Cosima Wagner's Diaries*, eds. Martin Gregor-Dellin and Dieter Mack, trans. Geoffrey Skelton, 2 vols. (New York and London: Collins, 1978–80)

Wagner, Richard, *Richard Wagner's Prose Works*, trans. and ed. William Ashton Ellis, 8 vols. (London: Routledge & Kegan Paul, 1892–99)

Wagner, Richard, *Selected Letters of Richard Wagner*, trans. and ed. Stewart Spencer and Barry Millington (London: J. M. Dent & Sons, 1987)

Williams, Simon, *Wagner and the Romantic Hero* (Cambridge: Cambridge University Press, 2004)

Wagner websites[*]

In English or with an English-language option

Bayreuth Festival	www.bayreuther-festspiele.de
Richard Wagner Museum, Bayreuth	www.wahnfried.de
Richard-Wagner-Verband	www.richard-wagner-verband.de
Wagner Society UK	www.wagnersociety.org
Wagner Society New York	www.wagnersocietyny.org
The Wagner Journal	www.thewagnerjournal.co.uk
Wagner Opera	www.wagneropera.net
Wagner discographies	www.wagnerdiscography.com

[*] Links valid at the time of publication in 2012.

Note on the Contributors

Mike Ashman is an opera director whose productions include *Parsifal*, *Der fliegende Holländer* and the Norwegian premiere of *Der Ring des Nibelungen*. He has contributed to *Wagner in Performance*, *The Cambridge Companion to Wagner*, *The Cambridge Wagner Encyclopedia*, *Gramophone* and *Opera*.

John Deathridge is King Edward VII Professor of Music at King's College London and is a former president of the Royal Musical Association. He is the co-author of *The New Grove Wagner*. Recent publications on Wagner include a new critical edition of *Lohengrin* and *Wagner beyond Good and Evil*.

Katherine Syer teaches musicology and theatre history at the University of Illinois. Her work on the stage history of Wagner's works and his development as a dramatist has appeared in *Wagner and His World*, *A Companion to Wagner's 'Parsifal'*, *The Wagner Journal* and *Musical Quarterly*.

William Vaughan is Emeritus Professor of History of Art at Birkbeck College, University of London. His main area of research is Romanticism, particularly British and German art around 1800. His publications include *German Romanticism and English Art* and *Caspar David Friedrich*.

John Warrack was formerly Lecturer in Music at Oxford University. His publications include the Cambridge Opera Handbook on *Die Meistersinger von Nürnberg* and a history, *German Opera: From the Beginnings to Wagner*.

Acknowledgements

We would like to thank John Allison of *Opera*, Mike Ashman, Charles Johnston, Lionel Friend and Barry Millington for their assistance and advice in the preparation of this guide.